Rebound 19

This book may be kept

FOUR

HOME UNIVERSITY LIBRARY

OF MODERN KNOWLEDGE

No. 59

A complete classified list of the volumes of THE HOME UNIVERSITY LIBRARY *already published will be found at the back of this book.*

DR. JOHNSON AND HIS CIRCLE

BY

JOHN BAILEY

AUTHOR OF "POETS AND POETRY," "THE CLAIMS OF
FRENCH POETRY," ETC.

NEW YORK
HENRY HOLT AND COMPANY

LONDON
WILLIAMS AND NORGATE

CONTENTS

DR. JOHNSON AND
HIS CIRCLE

CHAPTER I

JOHNSON AS A NATIONAL INSTITUTION

THE name of Samuel Johnson is, of course,
not the greatest in English prose, but even
to-day, when he has been dead more than a
century and a quarter, it is still the most
familiar. We live in an age of newspapers.
Where all can read, the newspaper press, taken
as a whole, will be a fairly accurate reflection
of what is in the mind of a people. Nothing
will be mentioned frequently in newspapers
which is not of some interest to a large number
of readers; and whatever is frequently mentioned there cannot fail to become widely
known. Tried by this test, Johnson's name
must be admitted to be very widely known
and of almost universal interest. No man
of letters—perhaps scarcely even Shakespeare
himself—is so often quoted in the columns
of the daily press. His is a name that may

7

10308

be safely introduced into any written or spoken discussion, without fear of the stare of unrecognizing ignorance; and the only danger to which those who quote him expose themselves is that of the yawn of over-familiarity. Even in his own lifetime his reputation extended far beyond the limited circle of literature or scholarship. Actresses delighted in his conversation; soldiers were proud to entertain him in their barracks; innkeepers boasted of his having slept in their inns. His celebrity was such that he himself once said there was hardly a day in which the newspapers did not mention his name; and a year after his death Boswell could venture to write publicly of him that his " character, religious, moral, political and literary, nay his figure and manner, are, I believe, more generally known than those of almost any man." But what was, in his own day, partly a respect paid to the maker of the famous *Dictionary* and partly a curiosity about " the great Oddity," as the Edensor innkeeper called him, has in the course of the nineteenth century become a great deal more.

He is still for us the great scholar and the strongly marked individuality, but he has gradually attained a kind of apotheosis, a kind of semi-legendary position, almost rivalling that of the great John Bull himself, as the embodiment of the essential features of the English character. We never think of the typical Englishman being like Shakespeare or Milton. In the first place, we know very little about Shakespeare, and not very much about Milton; and so we are thrown back on their works, and our mental picture of them takes on a dim and shadowy grandeur, very unlike what we see when we look within into our familiar and commonplace selves. Nor do Englishmen often plume themselves on their æsthetic or imaginative gifts. The achievements of Wren, or Purcell, or Keats may arouse in them admiration and pride, but never a sense of kinship. When they recognize themselves in the national literature, it is not Hamlet, or Lear, or Clarissa, or Ravenswood that holds up the mirror; but Falstaff, or The Bastard, or Tom Jones, or Jeanie Deans, or perhaps Gabriel Oak: plain people, all of them, whatever their differences, with a certain quiet and downright quality which Englishmen are apt to think the peculiar birthright of the people of this island. It is that quality which was the central thing in the mind of Johnson, and it is to his possession of it, and to our unique knowledge of it through Boswell, that more than anything else he owes this position of the typical Englishman among our men of letters. We can all imagine that under other conditions, and with an added store of brains and character, we might each have been Doctor Johnson. Before we could fancy ourselves Shelley or Keats the self that we know would have to be not developed but destroyed. But in Johnson we see our own magnified and glorified selves.

It has sometimes been asserted to be the function of the man of letters to say what others can feel or think but only he can express. Whatever may be thought of such a definition of literature, it is certain that Johnson discharged this particular function with almost unique success. And he continues to do so still, especially in certain fields. Whenever we feel strongly the point of view of common sense we almost expect to be able to find some trenchant phrase of Johnson's with which to express it. If it cannot be found it is often invented. A few years ago, a lover of Johnson walking along a London street passed by the side of a cabmen's shelter. Two cabmen were getting their dinner ready, and the Johnsonian was amused and pleased to hear one say to the other : "After all, as Doctor Johnson says, a man may travel all over the world without seeing anything better than his dinner." The saying was new to him and probably apocryphal, though the sentiment is one which can well be imagined

as coming from the great man's mouth. But
whether apocryphal or authentic, the remark
well illustrates both the extent and the particular nature of Johnson's fame. You would
not find a cabman ascribing to Milton or Pope
a shrewd saying that he had heard and liked.
Is there any man but Johnson in all our literary history whom he would be likely to call
in on such an occasion ? That is the measure
of Johnson's universality of appeal. And
the secret of it lies, to use his own phrase, not
used of himself of course, in the " bottom of
sense," which is the primary quality in all he
wrote and said, and is not altogether absent
from his ingrained prejudices, or even from
the perversities of opinion which his love of
argument and opposition so constantly led
him to adopt. Whether right or wrong there
is always something broadly and fundament-
ally human about him which appeals to all and
especially to the plain man. Every one feels
at home at once with a man who replies to
doubts about the freedom of the will with the
plain man's answer : " Sir, we *know* our will's
free, and there's an end on't," and if he adds
to it an argument which the plain man would
not have thought of, it is still one which the
plain man and everyone else can understand.
" You are surer that you can lift up your finger
or not as you please, than you are of any

conclusion from a deduction of reasoning."
Moreover we all think we are more honest than
our neighbours and are at once drawn to the
man who was less of a humbug than any man
who ever lived. "Clear your mind of cant"
is perhaps the central text of Johnson, on which
he enlarged a hundred times. "When a
butcher tells you his heart bleeds for his
country, he has in fact no uneasy feeling."
No one who has ever attended an election
meeting fails to welcome that saying, or the
answer to Boswell's fears that if he were in
Parliament he would be unhappy if things
went wrong, "That's cant, sir. . . . Public
affairs vex no man." "Have they not vexed
yourself a little, sir ? Have you not been
vexed at all by the turbulence of this reign
and by that absurd vote of the House of
Commons, 'That the influence of the Crown
has increased, is increasing, and ought to
be diminished' ? " "Sir, I have never slept
an hour less, nor eat an ounce less meat. I
would have knocked the factious dogs on
the head, to be sure; but I was not *vexed*."

Here we all know where we are. This is what
we wish we could have said ourselves, and
can fancy ourselves saying under more favourable circumstances; and we like the man who
says it for us. Certainly no man, not even
Swift, ever put the plain man's view with

such exactness, felicity, and force as Johnson does a thousand times in the pages of
Boswell. And not only in the pages of Boswell.
One of the objects of this introductory chapter
is to try to give a preliminary answer to the
very natural question which confronts every
one who thinks about Johnson, how it has
come about that a man whose works are so
little read to-day should still be so great a
name in English life. How is it that in this
HOME UNIVERSITY LIBRARY he is the second
author to have a volume to himself, only
Shakespeare preceding him ? The primary
answer is, of course, that we know him, as we
know no other man whose face we never saw,
whose voice we never heard. Boswell boasted
that he had " Johnsonized the land," and
that he had shown Johnson in his book as no
man had ever been shown in a book before :
and the boast is after a hundred years seen
to be a literal statement of fact. But after
all Boswell did not make Johnson's reputation.
On the contrary, it was Johnson's name that
sold Boswell's book. No man owes so much
to his biographer as Johnson to Boswell, but
that must not make us forget that Johnson
was the most famous man of letters in England
before he ever saw Boswell. Boswell's earnest
desire to make his acquaintance and to sit
humbly at his feet was only an extreme in-

stance of an attitude of respect and admiration, often even of reverence, commonly felt towards him among the more intelligent and serious portion of the community. He had not then attained to the position of something like Dictatorship which he filled in the world of English letters at the time he wrote the *Lives of the Poets*, but, except the *Shakespeare* and the *Lives*, all the work that gave him that position was already done. In this case, as in others, fame increased in old age without any corresponding increase in achievement, and it was the easy years at Streatham, not the laborious years at Gough Square, that saw him honoured and courted by bishops and judges, peers and commoners, by the greatest of English statesmen and the greatest of English painters. But his kingship was in him from the first. He had been ἄναξ ἀνδρῶν even among his schoolfellows. His bigness, in more ways than one, made them call him " the great boy," and the father of one of them was astute enough even then to perceive that he would be more than that: " you call him the great boy, but take my word for it, he will one day prove a great man." The boys looked upon him so much as a superior being to themselves that three of them, of whom one was his friend Hector, whom he often saw in later life, " used to come in the morning as his humble attendants and carry him to school. One in the middle stooped while he sat upon his back, and one on each side supported him, and thus he was borne triumphant." Such a tribute by boys to intellectual superiority was less rare in those days than it has become since : but it would not be easy to find a parallel to it at any time. What began at school continued through life. Even when he was poorest and most obscure, there was something about him that secured respect. It is too little to say that no one ever imagined he could with impunity behave disrespectfully to Johnson. No one ever dared to do so. As he flung the well-meant boots from his door at Oxford, so throughout life he knew how to make all men afraid to insult, slight, or patronize him.

But these, after all, were qualities that would only affect the few who came into personal contact with him. What was it that affected the larger world and gave him the fame and authority of his later years ? Broadly speaking of course it was what he had written, the work he had done, his poems, his *Rambler* and *Idler*, his *Rasselas*, his *Shakespeare*, above all that colossal and triumphant piece of single-handed labour, the *Dictionary of the English Language*. But there was more than that. Another man might have written

books quite as valuable, and attained to
nothing like Johnson's position. A thousand
people to-day read what Gray was writing in
those years for one who reads what Johnson
wrote, and they are quite right. Yet Gray in
his lifetime had little fame and no authority
except among his friends. Pope, again, had
of course immense celebrity, more no doubt
than Johnson ever had among men of letters ;
but he never became, as Johnson did, something almost like a national institution. What
was it that gave Johnson what great poets
never attained ? It could not yet be his
reputation as a great talker, which was only
beginning to spread. We think of him as the
greatest talker the world has ever seen : but
that is chiefly due to Boswell, of course, and
we are speaking at present of the years before
the memorable meeting in the back parlour
of Mr. Davies's shop in Russell Street, Covent
Garden. Besides, good talk, except in Boswell's pages, is like good acting, a vain thing
to those who only know it by hearsay. We
are therefore thrown back on Johnson's public
work for an explanation of the position he
held. What was it in his work, with so little
of Pope's amazing wit and brilliancy, with
so little of Gray's fine imaginative quality
and distinction, prose too, 'in the main, and
not poetry, with none of the prestige of poetry

that gave him what neither Pope nor Gray
ever received, what it is scarcely too much
to call, the homage of a nation ?

The answer is that, especially in England,
it is not brillance or distinction of mind that
win the respect of a nation. George III had
many faults, but all through his reign he was
an admirable representative of the general
feelings of his people. And he never did a
more representative act than when he gave
Johnson a pension, or when he received him
in the library of Buckingham House. No
doubt many, though not all, of Johnson's
political and ecclesiastical prejudices were
very congenial to the king, but plenty of
people shared George III's views without
gaining from him an ounce of respect. What
he and the nation dimly felt about Johnson
was a quality belonging less to the author than
to the man. The English, as we were saying
just now, think of themselves as a plain people,
more honest and direct in word and deed than
the rest of the world. George III never
affected to be anything but a plain man, was
very honest according to his lights, and never
for an instant failed to have the courage of
his convictions. Such a king and such a
people would inevitably be attracted to a man
of Johnson's fearless sincerity and invincible
common sense. The ideal of the nation is

B

still the same. Johnson once praised the third Duke of Devonshire for his " dogged veracity." We have lately seen one of that duke's descendants and successors, a man of no obvious or shining talents, attain to a position of almost unique authority among his fellow countrymen mainly by his signal possession of this hereditary gift of veracity, honesty and good sense. So it was with Johnson himself. Behind all his learning lay something which no learned language could conceal. " On s'attend à voir un auteur et on trouve un homme." Authors then, as now, were often thought to be fantastical, namby-pamby persons, living in dreams, sharing none of the plain man's interests, eager and querulous about trifles and unrealities, indifferent and incapable in the broad world of life. Nobody could feel that about Johnson.

He never pretended to be superior to the pains or pleasures of the body and never concealed his interest in the physical basis of life. He might with truth have spoken, as Pope did, of " that long disease, my life," for he declares in one of his letters that after he was past twenty his health was such that he seldom enjoyed a single day of ease; and he was so scrupulously truthful when he had a pen in his hand that that must be taken as at the least a literal record of the truth as it appeared to him at that moment. But though he never enjoyed health he never submitted to the tyranny of disease. The manliness that rings through all he wrote made itself felt also in his life, and we are not surprised to hear from Mrs. Thrale, in whose house he lived so long, that he "required less attendance sick or well than ever I saw any human creature." He could conquer disease and pain, but he never affected stoic "braveries," about not finding them very actual and disagreeable realities. In the same way, he never pretended not to enjoy the universal pleasures, such as food and sleep. Boswell records him as saying: "Some people have a foolish way of not minding, or pretending not to mind, what they eat. For my part, I mind my belly very studiously and very carefully, for I look upon it that he who does not mind his belly will hardly mind anything else." This is not particularly refined language, and Johnson's manners at the dinner-table, where, until he had satisfied his appetite, he was "totally absorbed in the business of the moment," were not always of a nature to please refined people. But our present point is that they were only an exaggeration of that sense of bodily realities which is one of the things that has always helped to secure for him the plain man's confidence. Throughout his life he kept his feet firmly based on the solid ground of fact. Human life, as it is actually and visibly lived, was the subject of his study and conversation from first to last. He always put fine-spun theories to mercilessly positive tests such as the ordinary man understands and trusts at once, though ordinary men have not the quickness or clearness of mind to apply them. When people preached a theory to him he was apt to confute them simply by applying it to practice. He supposed them to act upon it, and its absurdity was demonstrated. One of his friends was Mrs. Macaulay, who was a republican and affected doctrines of the equality of all men. When Johnson was at her house one day he put on, as he says, " a very grave countenance," and said to her : " Madam, I am now become a convert to your way of thinking. I am convinced that all mankind are upon an equal footing; and to give you an unquestionable proof, madam, that I am in earnest, here is a very sensible, civil, well-behaved fellow-citizen, your footman : I desire that he may be allowed to sit down and dine with us." No wonder that, as he adds, " she has never liked me since." To the political thinker, perhaps, such an argument rather proves the insincerity of Mrs. Macaulay than what he claimed for it, " the absurdity of the levelling doctrine." But it exhibits, with a force that no theoretical reasoning could match, the difficulty which doctrines of equality will always have to meet in the resistance of human nature as it is and as it is likely to remain for a long time to come. And it illustrates the habit of Johnson's mind which has always made the unlearned hear him so gladly, the habit of forcing theory to the test of fact. For quick as he was, perhaps quicker than any recorded man, at the tierce and quart of theoretical argument, he commonly used the bludgeon stroke of practice to give his opponent the final blow. We are vaguely distrustful of our reasoning powers, but every man thinks he can understand facts and figures. The quickness of Johnson in applying arithmetical tests to careless statements must have been another of the elements the fear, respect and confidence he inspired. A gentleman once told him that in France, as soon as a man of fashion marries, he takes an opera girl into keeping, and he declared this to be the general custom. " Pray, sir," said Johnson, " how many opera girls may there be ? " He answered, " About four score." " Well then, sir," replied Johnson, " you see there can be no more than fourscore men of fashion who can do this."

There is no art of persuasion, as all orators know, so overwhelming in effect as this appeal, or even appearance of appeal, to a court in which every man feels as much at home as the speaker himself. And though Johnson's use of it is, of course, seen at its most telling in his conversation, it was in him from the first, is a conspicuous feature of all he wrote, and was undoubtedly a powerful factor in winning for him the reputation of manliness and honesty he enjoyed. Take, for instance, a few paragraphs from his analysis of the rhetoric of authors on the subject of poverty. It is No. 202 of *The Rambler*. There is no better evidence of his perfect freedom from that slavery to words which is the besetting sin of authors.

" There are few words of which the reader believes himself better to know the import than of *poverty ;* yet whoever studies either the poets or philosophers will find such an account of the condition expressed by that term as his experience or observation will not easily discover to be true. Instead of the meanness, distress, complaint, anxiety and dependence, which have hitherto been combined in his ideas of poverty, he will read of content, innocence and cheerfulness, of health and safety, tranquillity and freedom; of pleasures not known but to men unencumbered with possessions; and of sleep that sheds his balsamick anodynes only on the cottage. Such are the blessings to be obtained by the resignation of riches, that kings might descend from their thrones and generals retire from a triumph, only to slumber undisturbed in the elysium of poverty."

.   .   .   .   .

" But it will be found upon a nearer view that they who extol the happiness of poverty do not mean the same state with those who deplore its miseries. Poets have their imaginations filled with ideas of magnificence; and being accustomed to contemplate the downfall of empires, or to contrive forms of lamentation for monarchs in distress, rank all the classes of mankind in a state of poverty who make no approaches to the dignity of crowns. To be poor, in the epick language, is only not to command the wealth of nations, nor to have fleets and armies in pay.

" Vanity has perhaps contributed to this impropriety of style. He that wishes to become a philosopher at a cheap rate easily gratifies his ambition by submitting to poverty when he does not feel it, and by boasting his contempt of riches when he has already more than he enjoys. He who would show the extent of his views and grandeur of his conceptions, or discover his acquaintance with splendour and magnificence, may talk, like Cowley, of an humble station and quiet obscurity, of the paucity of nature's wants, and the inconveniences of superfluity, and at last, like him, limit his desires to five hundred pounds a year; a fortune indeed, not exuberant, when we compare it with the expenses of pride and luxury, but to which it little becomes a philosopher to affix the name of poverty, since no man can with any propriety be termed poor who does not see the greater part of mankind richer than himself."

What good sense, what resolute grip on the realities of life, what a love of truth and seriousness, shines through the long sentences! The form and language of the essay may perhaps be too suggestive of the professional author; but how much the opposite, how very human and real, is the stuff and substance of what he says! Professor Raleigh once proposed as a test of great literature, that it should be found applicable and useful in circumstances very different from those that were in the author's mind when he wrote. By that test these words of Johnson are certainly great literature. The degrees of wealth and poverty have varied infinitely in the history of the world. They were very different under the Roman Empire from what they became in the Middle Age; by Johnson's day they had become quite unlike what they had been in

the days of Dante and Chaucer; and they
have again changed almost or quite as much
in the hundred and thirty years that have
passed since he died. Yet was there ever
a time, will there ever be, when the self-
deception of the human heart or the loose
thinking of the human mind, will not allow
men who never knew poverty to boast of
their cheerful endurance of it ? Have we
not to-day reached a time when men with an
assured income of ten, twenty, or even thirty
pounds a week, affect to consider themselves
too poor to be able to afford to marry ? And
where will such people better find the needed
recall to fact, than in Johnson's trenchant
and unanswerable appeal to the obvious
truth as all can see it, if they will, for themselves, in the visible conditions of the world
about them: " No man can, with any propriety, be termed poor who does not see the
greater part of mankind richer than himself ? "

This hold on the realities of life is the most
essential element in Johnson's greatness.
Ordinary people felt it from the first, however
unconsciously, and looked to Johnson as
something more than an author. Pope might
do himself honour by acclaiming the verses
of the unknown poet : Warburton might hasten
to pay his tribute to the unknown critic : but
they could not give Johnson, what neither

of them could have gained for himself, the
confidence, soon to be felt by the whole
reading part of the population of England,
that here was a man uniquely rich in the
wisdom of every day, learned but no victim
of learning, sincerely religious but with a
religion that never tried to ignore the facts
of human life, a scholar, a philosopher and
a Christian, but also pre-eminently a man.

A grave man, no doubt, apt to deal in
grave subjects, especially when he had his
pen in his hand. But that helped rather than
hindered his influence. He would not have
liked to think that he owed part of his own
authority to the sixteenth and seventeenth
century Puritans, but no doubt he did. Still
the Puritan movement only deepened a
vein of seriousness which had been in the
English from Saxon days. One may see it
everywhere. The Puritans would not have
been the power they were if they had not
found congenial soil in the English character.
The Reformation itself, a Protestant may be
excused for thinking, owes its ultimate
triumph in England partly to the fact that
Englishmen saw in it a movement towards a
more serious and ethical religion than the
Catholicism either of the Middle Age or of
the Jesuits. The same thing may be seen in
the narrower fields of literature. The Renais-

sance on the whole takes a much more ethical note in England than, for instance, in France. A little later indeed, in the France of Pascal and Bossuet, books of devotion and theology were very widely read, as may be seen in the letters of Madame de Sévigné; but they can never have had anything like the circulation which they had in England, both in the seventeenth and eighteenth centuries. Every one who looks at an English country-house library is struck by the abundant provision of sermons, mainly collected, like everything else indeed, in the eighteenth century. And every reader of Boswell's *Johnson* has been impressed by the frequent recurrence of devotional and religious books in the literary talk of the day, and, what is perhaps more remarkable, by the fact that wherever Boswell and Johnson go they constantly find volumes of sermons lying about, not only in the private houses, but also in the inns where they stay. There never was a period when " conduct," as Matthew Arnold used to call it, was so admitted to be the three-fourths of life he claimed for it, as it was between the Restoration and the French Revolution. It was conduct, not faith, ethics not religion, the " whole duty of man " in this life, not his supernatural destiny in another, that mainly occupied the minds of serious people in that unecclesiastical age. And Johnson, definite Christian, definite Churchman as he was, full even of ecclesiastical prejudices, was just the man to appeal to a generation with such interests as these.

No questions occupied him so much as moral questions. He was all his life considering how he ought to live, and trying to live better. People who are in earnest about these things have always found not only his published prayers or his moral essays, but his life as told by Boswell full of fortifying and stimulating ethical food. All alike exhibit a mind that recognized the problem of the conduct of life as the one thing of supreme interest to a rational man, and recognized it as above all things a moral problem. His treatment of it is usually based on reason, not on mere authority or orthodoxy, or even on Christianity at all. *Rasselas*, for instance, his most popular ethical work, which was translated into most of the European languages, does not contain a single allusion to Christianity. Its atmosphere is neither Mahomedan nor Christian, but that of pure reason. And when elsewhere he does discuss definitely Christian problems it is usually in the light of free and unfettered reason. Reason by itself has probably never made any one a Christian, and certainly Johnson's

Christianity was not an affair of the reason alone, but he was seldom afraid to test it by the touchstone of reason. That was not merely a thing done in accordance with the fashion of his age; it was the inevitable activity of an acute and powerful mind. But the fact that he had in him this absorbing ethical interest, and that throughout his life he was applying to it a rare intellectual energy, and what was rarer still in those fields, a close and unfailing grip on life and reality, gave him that peculiar position to which he came in his last years; one of an authority which was probably not equalled by that of any professed philosopher or divine.

Still, his seriousness could not by itself have given him this position. The English people like their public men to be serious, but they do not like them to be nothing else. The philosopher and the saint, the merely intellectual man or the merely spiritual man, have never been popular characters or become leaders of men, here any more than elsewhere. The essential element in the confidence Johnson inspired was not his seriousness : it was his sovereign sanity, the unfailing common sense, to which allusion has already been made. He was pre-eminently a bookish man, but he was conspicuously free from the unreality that is so often felt in the characters of such men. He knew from the first how to strike a note which showed that he was well aware of the difference between literature and life and their relative importance.

" Deign on the passing world to turn thine eyes,
  And pause awhile from Letters, to be wise."

So he said, as a young man, in his finest poem, and so he acted all through the years. Scholar as he was, and very conscious of the dignity of scholarship, he never forgot that scholarship faded into insignificance in presence of the greater issues of life. In his most scholarly moment, in the Preface to the *Dictionary*, he will throw out such a remark as " this recommendation of steadiness and uniformity (in spelling) does not proceed from an opinion that particular combinations of letters have much influence on human happiness." Such a sentence could not but give plain people a feeling of unusual confidence in the writer. How different they would at once feel it to be, how different, indeed, we still feel it, from the too frequent pedantry of critics, insisting with solemn importance or querulous ill-temper upon trifling points of grammar or style. We know that this man has a scale of things in his mind;

he will not vilify his opponent's character for
the sake of a difference about a Greek construction, or make a lifelong quarrel over
the question of the maiden name and birth-
place of Shelley's great-grandmother. From
first to last he was emphatically a human
being, with a feeling for human life as a
whole, and in all its parts. He said once :
" A mere antiquarian is a rugged being,"
and he was never himself a mere grammarian
or a mere scholar, but a man with an eager
interest in all the business and pleasure of
life. His high sense of the dignity of literature looked to its large and human side, not
to any parade of curious information. Everywhere in his writings plain people are concili-
ated by his frank attitude as to his own calling,
by his perfect freedom from any pontifical
airs of the mystery of authorship. " I could
have written longer notes," he says in the
great Preface to his *Shakespeare*, " for the
art of writing notes is not of difficult attain-
ment." " It is impossible for an expositor
not to write too little for some, and too much
for others." " I have indeed disappointed
no opinion more than my own; yet I have
endeavoured to perform my task with no
slight solicitude. Not a single passage in
the whole work has appeared to me corrupt
which I have not attempted to restore; or

obscure which I have not endeavoured to illustrate. In many I have failed, like others, and from many, after all my efforts, I have retreated, and confessed the repulse. I have not passed over with affected superiority what is equally difficult to the reader and to myself, but where I could not instruct him have owned my ignorance. I might easily have accumulated a mass of seeming learning upon easy scenes; but it ought not to be imputed to negligence that, where nothing was necessary, nothing has been done, or that, where others have said enough, I have said no more."

A man who writes like this is sure of his public at once. He is instantly seen to be too proud, as well as too sincere, too great a man, in fact, altogether, to stoop to the dishonest little artifices by which vanity tries to steal applause. In his writings as in his talk, he was not afraid to be seen for what he actually was; and just as, when asked how he came to explain the word Pastern as meaning the knee of a horse, he replied at once, "Ignorance, madam, pure ignorance," so in his books he made no attempt to be thought wiser or more learned than he was. And this modesty which he showed for himself he showed for his author too. The common notion that he depreciated

Shakespeare is, indeed, an entire mistake. There were certainly things in Shakespeare which were out of his reach, but that does not alter the fact that Shakespeare has never been better praised than in Johnson's Preface. But he will not say what he does not mean about Shakespeare any more than about himself. There is in him nothing at all of the subtle trickery of the common critic who thinks to magnify his own importance by extravagant and insincere laudation of his author. He is not afraid to speak of the poet with the same simplicity as he speaks of the editor. " Yet it must be at last confessed that, as we owe everything to him, he owes something to us; that, if much of his praise is paid by perception and judgment, much is likewise given by custom and veneration." He even adds that Shakespeare has " perhaps not one play which, if it were now exhibited as the work of a contemporary writer, would be heard to the conclusion." Whether that is true or not of Johnson's day or of our own—and let us not be too hastily sure of its untruth—at least the man who wrote it in the preface to an edition of Shakespeare lacked neither honesty nor courage. And he had then, as he has still, the reward which the most popular of the virtues will always bring.

C

With courage and honesty usually go simplicity and directness. That is not the first praise that Johnson would win from people familiar with caricatures of his style. But it is a complete mistake to suppose that he always wore that heavy armour of magniloquence. He could be as free from pedantry of phrase as he always was from pedantry of thought. He is not only a supreme master of common sense; he is a supreme master of the language of common sense. He has the gift of saying things which no one can misunderstand and no one can forget. His common sense is what its name implies, no private possession thrust upon the minds of others, but their own thoughts expressed for them. That was one of the secrets of the unique confidence he inspired. The jury gave him their verdict because he always put the issue on a basis they could understand. His answer to the specious arguments of the learned is always an appeal to what it needs no learning to know. The critics of Pope's *Homer* are met by the unanswerable retort : " To a thousand cavils one answer is sufficient. The purpose of a writer is to be read." To Pope himself affecting scorn of the great, the same merciless measure of common knowledge is dealt. " His scorn of the great is too often repeated to be real : no man thinks

much of that which he despises." And so
once more to Pope's victims. If they would
have kept quiet, he says, the *Dunciad* would
have been little read : " For whom did it
concern to know that one or another scribbler
was a dunce ? " But this is what the dunces
are the last people to realize : indeed, " every
man is of importance to himself, and therefore,
in his own opinion, to others "; so the victim
is the first to " publish injuries or misfortunes
which had never been known unless related
by himself, and at which those that hear
them will only laugh; for no man sympathizes
with the sorrows of vanity."

Every one who is much read in Johnson
will recall for himself other and perhaps
better instances than these of his rare faculty
of gathering together into a sentence some
piece of the common stock of wisdom or
observation, and applying it simply, directly
and unanswerably to the immediate business
in hand. Is there anything which clears and
relieves an argument so well ? " The true
state of every nation is the state of common
life "; " If one was to think constantly of
death the business of life would stand still ";
" To be happy at home is the ultimate result
of all ambition." How firm on one's feet, on
the solid ground of truth, one feels when one
reads such sentences ! The writer of them

C 2

is at once recognized as no maker of phrases, no victim of cloudy speculations, self-deceived and the deceiver of others, but a man who kept himself always close to the realities of things. And when to this, which had been always there, was added the special charm of the *Lives of the Poets*, the old man speaking, often in the first person, without reserve or mystery, out of the fullness of his knowledge of books and men and the general life which is greater than either, then the feeling entertained for him grew into something not very unlike affection. The man who could not be concealed even by the grave abstractions of the earlier works, was now seen and heard as a friend speaking face to face with those who understood him. The wisdom, and learning and piety, the shrewdness and vigour and wit, the invincible common sense, took visible shape in the face of Samuel Johnson, were heard in his audible voice, became known and honoured and loved as a kind of national glory, the embodiment of the mind and character of the English people. And then, of course, came Boswell. And what might have died away as a memory or a legend was made secure from mortality by a work of genius. At the moment Boswell had only to complete an impression already made. But, strong as it was at the time, without Boswell it could

not have lasted. Those who had sat with
Johnson at the Mitre or "The Club" could
not long survive, and could not leave their
eyes and ears behind them. Literary fashions
changed; popular taste began to ask ever-
more for amusement and less for instruction
or edification; and the works of Johnson
were no longer read, except by students of
English literature. But for Boswell the great
man's name might soon have been unknown
to any but bookish men. It is due to Boswell
that journalists quote him, and cabmen tell
stories about him. Johnson had himself
almost every quality that makes for survival
except genius; and that, by the happiest of
fates for himself and for us, he found in his
biographer.

CHAPTER II

THE GENIUS OF BOSWELL

THE word genius seems a strange one to
apply to Boswell. Macaulay has had his
hour of authority with most of us, and,
unluckily for him and for us, the worst passages
in his *Essays* are often better remembered

than the greatest chapters in his *History*. It has proved his ill-fortune as well as his glory to have written so vividly that the mind's eye will still see what he wrote clear before it, though twenty years may lie between it and the actual sight of the printed page. At his worst he is like an advertisement hoarding, crude, violent, vulgar, but impossible to escape. The essay on Croker's Boswell is one of those unfortunate moments. It is, unhappily, far better known than its author's article on Johnson written for the *Encyclopædia Britannica,* and its violence still takes the memory by assault. No one forgets the disgusting description of Johnson, or the insults heaped upon Boswell. Least of all can anybody forget the famous paradox about the contrast between Boswell and his book. As a biographer, according to Macaulay, Boswell has easily surpassed all rivals. "Homer is not more decidedly the first of Epic poets, Shakespeare is not more decidedly the first of dramatists, Demosthenes is not more decidedly the first of orators than Boswell is the first of biographers. He has no second. Eclipse is first, and the rest nowhere." And yet this same Boswell is "a man of the meanest and feeblest intellect"; and, strangest of all, only achieves his amazing success by force of his worthlessness and folly. "If he had not been a great fool he would never have been a great writer."

Macaulay was the most self-confident of men. But, though he set his opinion with assurance against that of any other critic, there was one verdict he respected, the verdict of time. He would not have been astonished to hear that in the eighty years since his essay was written the fame of Boswell's book has continually increased. But few things that have happened since then would have surprised him more than to be told that, in a volume published only fifty years after his death and in part officially addressed to his own University of Cambridge, a Professor of English Literature, one of the two or three universally acknowledged masters of criticism, would be found quietly letting fall, as a thing about which there need be no discussion, a sentence beginning with the words: "A wiser man than Macaulay, James Boswell."

It may be well, before speaking further of Johnson, to say something about the man to whom we owe most of our knowledge of him, the most important member of his circle, this same James Boswell. Like all good biographers, he has put himself into his book; and we know him as well as we know Johnson, as we know no other two men, perhaps, in the history of the world. It cannot be denied that, when we put his great book down, it is not very easy to follow Sir Walter Raleigh in talking of him as a wise man, or even as a wiser man than Macaulay. If Boswell and Macaulay were put into competition in a prize for wisdom, no ordinary examiners would give it to Boswell. By the only tests they could apply, Macaulay must far outstrip him. The wisdom which enabled Macaulay to render splendid services to the State and to literature, and gave him wealth, happiness, popularity and a peerage, is as easily tested, and, it must be confessed, as real, as the unwisdom which ended in Boswell dying the dishonoured death of a drunkard, and leaving a name of which his descendants felt the shame at least as much as the glory.

But there are other tests, and though their superior value may be doubted, they ought not to be altogether ignored. Macaulay, who knew everything and achieved so much, spent his whole life in visible and external activities— talking, reading, writing, governing; and was admired, and, indeed, admirable in them all. But of the wisdom which realizes how essentially inferior all measurable doing, however triumphant, is to being, which is immeasurable, the wisdom which is occupied with the ultimate issues of life and death, he had apparently as little as any man who ever lived. He seems always to have been one of those active, hurrying, useful persons who—

"Fancy that they put forth all their life
  And never know how with the soul it fares."

Whatever can be said against Boswell that cannot be said. Of this inner wisdom, this quietness of thought, this "folie des grandeurs" of the soul, he had a thousand times as much as Macaulay. He could not cling to it to the end, he could not victoriously live by it and make it himself; but he had seen the vision which Macaulay never saw, and he never altogether forgot it. Every man is partly a lost soul. So far as Boswell was that, he knew it in all the bitter certainty of tears. So far as Macaulay was, he was as unconscious of it as the beasts that perish. And the kingdom of wisdom, like the Kingdom of Heaven, is more easily entered by those who know that they are outside it, than by those who do not know that there is such a place and are quite content where they are.

But these are high matters into which there is no need to go further. It is necessary, however, to say a little more about Boswell's character and abilities. He and Johnson are now linked together for all eternity; and everybody who takes an interest in Johnson is interested in Boswell too. It ought to be

much more than interest, and in all true
Johnsonians it is. Without Boswell, we
should have respected Johnson, honoured
him as a man and a writer, liked him as " a
true-born Englishman," but we could not
have known him enough to love him. By the
help of Boswell, we can walk and talk with
him, dine with him, be with him at his prayers
as well as at his pleasures, laugh with him,
learn of him and disagree with him; above all,
love him as we only can love a human being,
and never a mere wise man or great writer.
No Englishman doubts that Boswell has given
us one of the great books of the world. But
before we realize its greatness, we realize
its pleasantness, its companionableness. The
Life of Johnson and the *Journal of a Tour to
the Hebrides* may be taken for practical
purposes as one book; and it has some claim
to be the most companionable book in the
world. There is no book like it for a solitary
meal. A novel, if it is good for anything, is
too engrossing for a dinner companion. It is
impossible to put it down. It interrupts the
business of dining and results in cold food and
indigestion. A book of short poems—the
Odes of Horace, the Fables of La Fontaine,
the Sonnets of Shakespeare or Wordsworth—
is much more to the purpose. One may read
an Ode or a Sonnet quickly and then turn

again to one's dinner, carrying the fine verse in one's mind and tasting it at leisure as one holds good wine in the mouth before letting it pass away into forgetfulness. But poetry is not for every man, nor for every mood of any man : and the moment of dinner is not with most men the moment when they appear most poetic either to others or to themselves.

But is there any time which is not the time for Boswell ? He does not ask for a mood which may not be forthcoming : he does not demand an attention which it is inconvenient to give. We can take him up and lay him down as and when we will. And he has everything in his store. If we are seriously inclined and wish to have something to think about when we turn from the book to the dinner, he is full of the most serious questions, discussed sometimes wisely, almost always by wise men, the problems of morals and politics, of religion and society and literature, such questions as those of liberty and necessity in philosophy, liberty and government in politics, the English Church and the Roman, private education and public, life in the country and life in the town. Or if we wish, not for problems of any kind, but just for a picture of life as it was lived a hundred and fifty years ago, there is nothing like Boswell's pages for variety, intimacy, veracity and,

what is the great point in these matters,
lavishness of detail. His book is sown with
apparently, but only apparently, insignificant
trifles. What and how Johnson ate, his
manner in talking and walking, the colour and
shape of his clothes, the size of his stick, all
these and a thousand similar details we know
from Boswell, and because Boswell had the
genius to perceive that they accumulate upon
us a sensation of life and bodily presence, as of
a man standing before our eyes.

So, again, with the many little stories he
tells which no one else would have told. Who
but he would have treasured up every word of
that curious meeting in April 1778, between
Johnson and his unimportant old friend
Edwards, the man who said that he had tried
to be a philosopher, but "cheerfulness was
always breaking in "? Yet it is not only one
of the most Boswellian but one of the very
best things in the whole book. It exactly
illustrates what was newest in his method.
In an age of generality and abstraction he saw
the advantage of the concrete and particular,
and put into practice the lesson his master
could only preach, "Nothing is too little for
so little a creature as man." So the total-
abstaining Johnson and the bibulous Reynolds
and Boswell will each come before us exactly
as they were : and we are amused as we picture

the confusion of Reynolds's distinguished
parties where the servants had never been
taught to wait, and make a note of the progress
of social manners as we sympathize with Johnson at Edinburgh throwing the fingered lump of
sugar out of the window.   Some people, again,
like Mr. Gladstone, are fond of observing and
discoursing upon the changes of taste in the
matter of wine : and such people will find in
Boswell almost as much to interest their
curiosity as Johnson's own fellowship of tea-
drinkers. The drinker of champagne will
have to accept the mere modernity of his
beverage, which finds no place in Johnson's
famous hierarchy : " Claret for boys, port for
men, brandy for heroes."   Or, once more, if
our meal ends in tobacco, we may please
ourselves by contemplating the alternate, but
never contemporaneous, glories of snuff and
tobacco, and note the sage's curious, but
strictly truthful, account of the advantages
and disadvantages of smoking. " Smoking
has gone out. To be sure it is a shocking
thing, blowing smoke out of our mouths into
other people's mouths, eyes, and noses, and
having the same thing done to us. Yet I
cannot account why a thing which requires
so little exertion and yet preserves the mind
from total vacuity has gone out."   Or if we
demand a keener relish for our meal than these

quiet joys of observation, there is of course the whole store of Johnson's sallies of wit, the things we all quote and forget and like to have recalled to us.

For all these reasons Boswell's book, stuffed full of matter, and such matter as you can take up and lay down at pleasure, is the ideal companion for the man who dines or sups alone. Provided, of course, that he has some tincture of intellectual tastes. Those whose curiosity is only awakened by a prospect of the "sporting tips" will not care for Boswell. For, though the book moves throughout in the big world, and not in an academic groove, it still always moves intellectually. It asks a certain acquaintance with literature and history and the life of the human mind. The talk may, indeed, be almost said to deal with all subjects; but it tends mainly to be of the kind which will come uppermost when able men of a serious and bookish turn congregate together. It requires leisure, and that sense of the value of talk which has grown rarer in the hurry of a generation in which the idlest people affect to be busy, and those who do nothing at all are in a bustle from morning till night. Johnson was never in a hurry, especially in the later days, when he had done his work and was enjoying his fame. Mrs. Thrale says that conversation was all he required to make him happy. He hated people who broke it up to go to bed or to keep an appointment. Much as he delighted in John Wesley's company, he complained that he was never at leisure, which, said Johnson, "is very disagreeable to a man who loves to fold his legs and have out his talk as I do." The world has perhaps grown a more industrious place since those days, though nobody yet has managed to put so much into twenty-four hours as Wesley did. Anyhow the conditions that made for such talk as fills Boswell's pages are no doubt less common to-day : and perhaps it only lingers now in some rare Common Room at Oxford or Cambridge, where the evil spirit of classes and examinations has been strictly exorcised, or in an exceptionally well-chosen party at an exceptional country house, or in the old dining societies of London, such as Johnson's own, "The Club," of famous memory. Its modern rarity may, however, only make it the more precious in a book, and it is certainly not the least important element in the popularity of Boswell's work.

That work has always been praised from the day of its appearance. Lord Thurlow, then Chancellor, wrote to Boswell of the *Tour to the Hebrides*, which is essentially, though not formally, its first instalment, that he had read every word of it, because he could not help it : and added the flattering question, ' Could you give a rule how to write a book that a man *must* read ? " Scott, a little later, spoke of it as " without exception the best parlour window book that ever was written." Six editions were issued within twenty years of its appearance, a strong proof of popularity in the case of a voluminous and expensive book. And the praise and popularity have gone on growing ever since. But the strange thing is that the man who wrote it has commonly been treated with insult, and even with contempt. The fact is at first sight so inexplicable that it is worth a little looking into. A man who has done us all such a service as Boswell, who has by the admission even of Macaulay utterly out-distanced all competition in such an important kind of literature as biography, would naturally have been loaded with the gratitude and admiration of posterity. Yet all fools and some wise men have thought themselves entitled to throw a scornful stone at Boswell.

The truth is that Boswell was a man of very obvious weaknesses, the weaknesses to which every fool feels himself superior, and of some grave vices of a sort to which wise men feel little temptation. And, unfortunately, he conquered neither. Rather they conquered him, and made his last years a degradation, and his memory one which his friends were glad to forget. After the death of Johnson in 1784, followed in 1789 by that of Mrs. Boswell, whom Johnson once justly and generously described as the prop and stay of her husband's life, he had no one left to lean on. And he was not a man strong enough to stand alone. But it is time to insist that, when all this has been confessed, we are very far from having told the whole truth about Boswell. The fact is that justice will never be fully done to his memory till Macaulay and some others have been called up from their graves to do penance for their arrogant unfairness. Carlyle did something, but not enough; and he stands almost alone. Yet after all, considering what we owe Boswell, if there be any blindness in our view of him, it surely ought to be blindness to his faults. We have heard enough and to spare of his vanity, his self-importance, his entire lack of dignity, his weakness for wine and worse things than wine. But we have heard very little, far too little, of the kindness and genuineness of the man's whole nature, the warmth of his friendships and the enthusiastic loyalty of his hero-worship, of the reverence for religion and the earnest desire after being a better man, which, though often defeated

D

by temptation, were profound and absolutely sincere.

The notion that a man who does not practise what he preaches is necessarily insincere, always called forth an angry protest from Johnson. "Sir," he broke out at Inverary to Mr. M'Aulay, the historian's grandfather, "are you so grossly ignorant of human nature, as not to know that a man may be very sincere in good principles without having good practice?" No doubt this was a doctrine which Boswell heard gladly: and Johnson may himself have been influenced in his zeal for it by his consciousness that, as he said when enforcing it on another occasion, he had himself preached better than he had practised. "I have, all my life long, been lying till noon: yet I tell all young men, and tell them with great sincerity, that nobody who does not rise early will ever do any good." But, however that may be, he is plainly right in the broad issue. Practice is the only absolute proof of sincerity: but defect in practice is no proof of insincerity. Certainly, no Christian can doubt that the struggling, even though falling, sinner is in at least as hopeful a condition as the complacent person whose principles and practice are fairly conformable to each other because both live only the dormant life of respectability and convention. However, no one in his senses will try to make a hero or a saint out of Boswell. He was, as has been already said, vain, a babbler, a wine-bibber, a man of frequently irregular and ill-governed life. But to judge a man fairly as a whole, you must set his achievements against his failures, and include his aspirations as well as the weakness which prevented their being realized. He may also reasonably ask to be tried by the standard of his contemporaries. If this larger and juster method of judgment be adopted, the unfairness with which Boswell has been treated becomes immediately obvious. After all vanity is more a folly than a crime, and pays its own immediate penalty as no other crime or folly does. The other faults of Boswell, especially drinking, were only too common in a century at the beginning of which Johnson remembered " all the decent people at Lichfield getting drunk every night," and at the end of which the most honoured and feared of English Prime Ministers could appear intoxicated in the House of Commons itself. Drunkenness has not deprived Pitt of the gratitude of England, and we may well be determined that, if we can help it, it shall not deprive Boswell. It is not his vices but his virtues that are notable and unusual. What was extraordinary in his or any other day was the generous enthusiasm which made a young Scotch laird deliberately determine that he would do something more with his life than shoot wildfowl or play cards, made him throw himself first with a curious mixture of vanity and genuine devotion to a noble cause into the Corsican struggle for liberty, and then, vain of his birth and fortune as he was, place himself at the feet, not of a duke or a minister, but of a man of low origin, rough exterior, and rougher manners, in whom he simply saw the best and wisest man he had known. That is not the action of either a bad man or a fool; and assuredly Boswell—in the essence of him—was neither the one nor the other.

The truth is that he had the strength and the weaknesses of a man of mobile and lively imagination. He would fancy his wife and children drowned or dead for no better reason than that he was not by them; he would dream of being a judge when he had scarcely got a brief, and imagine himself a minister when he had no prospect of getting into Parliament. Other people experience these day-dreaming vanities, but they do not talk or write about them. Boswell did; and we all laugh at him, especially the fools among us: the wiser part add some of the love that belongs to the common kinship of humanity wherever it puts off the mask, the love of which we feel something even for that gross old " bourgeois " Samuel Pepys, just because he laid out his whole secret self in black and white upon the paper. Moreover, Boswell's absurdities had their finer side. The dreamer of improbable disasters and impossible good fortunes is also the dreamer of high and perhaps unattainable ideals. Shall we count it nothing to his honour that, instead of sitting down contentedly among the boon companions of Ayrshire, he aspired to read the best books in the world, to know the wisest men, and in turn to do something himself that should not be forgotten ? And note that those aspirations were in large part realized. His intellectual tastes always remained among the keenest of his pleasures : he numbered among his friends the most famous writer of his day, the greatest poet, the greatest painter, the profoundest and most eloquent of all English statesmen ; and before he died his apparent failure in personal achievements was transformed into the success that means immortality by the production of a book which after the lapse of a century has many more readers than the works of his great friends whose superiority to himself he would never have dreamed of challenging.

And what did these great men think of him ? Did the people who knew him think him altogether a fool ? If the magistrates of his native county had thought him merely that they would hardly have chosen him their chairman. Nor would the Royal Academy who filled their honorary offices with such men as Johnson, Goldsmith, and Gibbon, have given them Boswell as a colleague if they had thought him altogether a fool. Reynolds, again, who was his friend through life, and left him £200 in his will to be expended on a picture to be kept for his sake, was not a man who took fools for his friends. Burke, who at first doubted his fitness for election at " The Club," became a great admirer of his wonderful good humour, and received him on his own account and without Johnson as a guest at Beaconsfield, where neither fools nor knaves were commonly welcomed. The whole story of the tour to the Hebrides shows the regard felt for him, as himself and not only as the son of his father or the companion of Johnson, by many of the most distinguished and cultivated men in Scotland. Johnson, the most veracious of men, says of him in Scotland : " There is no house where he is not received with kindness and respect " ; and on another occasion he declared that Boswell " never left a house without leaving a wish for his return."

But the most complete refutation of the worthlessness of Boswell is of course the friendship and love he won from Johnson himself. Assuredly, the standard of Johnson, in whose presence nobody dared to swear or talk loosely, was not a low one either morally or intellectually; yet we find him saying that he held Boswell " in his heart of hearts "; perhaps, indeed, he loved Boswell better than any of his friends. " My dear Boswell, I love you very much "; " My dear Boswell, your kindness is one of the pleasures of my life "; " Come to me, my dear Bozzy, and let us be as happy as we can." This is the way Johnson constantly wrote and spoke to him. And this was not merely because Boswell was " the best travelling companion in the world," or even because he was, what Johnson also called him, " a man who finds himself welcome wherever he goes and makes new friends faster than he can want them," but also for graver reasons. Johnson said once that most friendships were the result of caprice or chance, "mere confederacies in vice or leagues in folly," but he did not choose that his own should be of that sort. Beauclerk is the only one of his friends who was not a man of high character. His feeling for Boswell was not a love of vice or folly. He saw Boswell at his best, no doubt : but that best must have had very real and positive good qualities in it to win from Johnson such a remark as he makes in one of his letters : " Never, my dear sir, do you take it into your head to think that I do not love you; you may settle yourself in full confidence both of my love and my esteem; I love you as a kind man, I value you as a worthy man, and hope in time to reverence you as a man of exemplary piety. I hold you, as Hamlet has it, ' in my heart of hearts.' " And there is a still more remarkable tribute in the letter to John Wesley giving Boswell an introduction to him " because I think it very much to be wished that worthy and religious men should be acquainted with each other." Nothing can be more certain than that Johnson would not have written so often in such language as this of a man who was what Macaulay thought Boswell was. Well may the foolish editor of Boswell's letters to Temple, who takes Macaulay's view, talk of the difficulty of explaining how it came about that Boswell formed one of a society which included such men as Johnson and Burke. The truth is that on his theory and Macaulay's it is not explicable at all.

Less explicable still, on that view, is the admitted excellence of Boswell's book. Carlyle dismissed with just contempt the absurd paradox that the greatness of the book was due to the imbecility of the author. That is a theory which it would be waste of time to discuss. But it may be worth while to point out that other and more rational explanations of Boswell's success are also insufficient. His book is acknowledged to have originated a new type of biography. It was felt at once, and has been increasingly felt ever since, that Boswell is so direct and personal that beside him all other biographers seem impersonal and vague, that he is so intimate that he makes all others appear cold and distant, so lifelike that they seem shadowy, so true that they seem false. Now this has commonly been attributed to his habit of noting down on the spot and at the moment anything that struck him in Johnson's talk or doings; and to his perfect willingness to exhibit his own discomfitures so long as they served to honour or illustrate his hero. In this way people have talked of his one merit being faithfulness, and of his work as a succession of photographs. Now it is true enough that his veracity is a very great merit, and that no one was ever so literally veracious as he. But no number of facts, and no quintessence of accuracy in using them, will ever make a great book. Literature is an art, and nothing great in art has ever been done with facts alone. The greatness comes from the quality of mind that is set to work upon the facts. Consequently

the secret of the success of the *Life of Johnson*
is to be found in the exact opposite of the
assertion of Macaulay. For the truth is that
the acknowledged excellence of the book is
in exact proportion to the unacknowledged
literary gifts of its author.

The law for all works of art and literature
is the same. The fact is nothing unless the
artist can give it life. Life comes from human
personality. *Ars est homo additus naturae.*
Art, that is, is nature seen through a temperament, the facts seen by a particular mind.
The landscape into which the painter has
put nothing of his own personality is fitter
for a surveyor's office than for a picture
gallery. The portrait which gives nothing
but the sitter's face is as dull as a photograph.
Two portraits of the same man, two sketches
of the same valley, not only are, but ought
to be, quite different from each other. Nature,
the facts of the particular face or scene,
remain the same for both : but the two different
artists, each bringing their own personality,
produce different results, when the face or
scene has become that composite mixture of
man and nature, fact and mind, which is
art. And this is as true of all books which
are meant to be literature as of painting or
sculpture. The story of Electra is, broadly
speaking, the same for Aeschylus, Sophocles,

and Euripides : but each contributes to it
himself, and the result differs.   Virgil's tale
of Troy is not Homer's : Chaucer gives us
one Troilus and Cressida, and Shakespeare
another : the fable of the Fox and the Goat
takes prose from Phædrus and poetry from
La Fontaine.   So Pope's Homer is not Homer,
the thing in itself, the unrelated, absolute
Homer, but *Pope additus Homero ;* and it is
not Euripides pure and simple which is the
true account of certain beautiful modern
versions of Euripides, but *Euripidi additus
Murray.*

It may be objected that these are all
instances from poetry, where the truth aimed
at is rather general than particular.   And
this distinction is a real one.   The truth of
the *Aeneid* is its truth to human life as a
whole, not its accuracy in reporting the words
used on particular occasions by Dido and
Turnus, neither of whom may have ever
existed.   History and biography are, undoubtedly, on a different footing in this
respect, just as the artist who calls his picture
" Arundel Castle " or " Windermere " is not
in the same position of freedom as the painter
of an " Evening on the Downs."   But the
law of *homo additus naturae* still remains
true in this case as in the other, though its
application is modified.   It is true that a

man who pretends to give a representation of Arundel is not justified in adding to it a tower 300 feet high just because he happens himself to have a fancy for towers. But what he has to add, if his work is to be art at all, is the emotional mood, the exaltation, depression, excitement, or whatever it may be, which Arundel stirred in him, and by means of which he and the scene before him were melted into that unity of intensified life which is born of the marriage of nature and man and is what we call art. The next day another man takes his place, and the result, though still Arundel Castle, is an entirely different picture. So in the case of books. The same Socrates is seen in one way when we get that part of him which could unite with the personality of Xenophon, and in quite another when the union is with Plato. The English Civil War marries one side of itself to Clarendon, and another to Milton; and both have that relative truth which is all art wishes for, and which is indeed a greater thing, as having human life in it, than any absolute truth in itself which, if it were discoverable, would be pure science, as useful perhaps, but as dead, as the First Proposition of Euclid. The greatness of literature depends on the degree in which the dead matter of fact belonging to the

subject has been quickened into life by the
emotional, intellectual and imaginative power
of the writer. And this is true of historical
and biographical work as well as of poetry.

That is the point to be remembered about
Boswell, and to be set against his detractors.
His book is admittedly one of the most living
books in existence. That life can have come
from no one but the author. It is the
irrefutable proof of his genius. Life and
power do not issue, here any more than elsewhere, out of folly and nonentity. The *Life
of Johnson* is the result of the most intimate
and fertile union between biographer and his
subject which has ever occurred, and it gives
us in consequence more of the essence of both
than any other biography. Boswell brought
to it his own bustling activity and curiosity
from which it draws its vividness and variety :
he brought to it also his warm-hearted, half-
morbid emotionalism from which it derives
its many moving pages : he brought to it his
reverence for Johnson, which enabled him
to exhibit, as no other man could, that kingship and priesthood which was a real part,
though not the whole, of Johnson's relation
to his circle. We see Johnson in his pages
as the guide, philosopher and friend of all
who came in his way, the intellectual and
spiritual father of Boswell, the master of his

studies, the director of his conscience. Nobody else in that company saw as much of the true and great Johnson as Boswell's loving devotion enabled him to see; and when he came to write the life he put himself into it, with the result that the portrait of Johnson as posterity sees it, will never lose the halo of glory with which the Boswellian hero-worship crowned it for all time.

This was the all-important *homo additus naturae* part of Boswell's work : the setting his subject in the light of his own imaginative and emotional insight. But there was more than that. Boswell had not only the temperament of the artist : he had an artist's craftsmanship. The *Life* makes four large octavo volumes, each of some 500 pages, in the great Oxford Edition by Birkbeck Hill : and the *Tour to the Hebrides* makes a fifth. That is a big book : yet so perfect an artist is Boswell, that scarcely once for a single page in all the five volumes is the chief light turned in any direction except that of Johnson. Anybody who has even read, much more anybody who has written, a book of any length knows how difficult and rare an achievement it is to maintain perfect unity of subject, never to lose the sense of proportion, never to let side issues and secondary personages obstruct or conceal the main business in hand.

There is nothing of the kind in Boswell. Under his hand no episode is ever allowed to be more than an episode, no minor character ever occupies the centre of the stage. Whoever and whatever is mentioned is mentioned only in relation to Johnson. Many great men, greater some of them than his hero, are brought into his picture, but it is never upon them that the chief light is thrown. All the other figures, whoever they are, are here but attendants upon Johnson's greatness, foils to his wit, witnesses to his virtues, his friends or his foes, the subjects or victims of his talk, anything that you will in connection with him, but apart from him—nothing. All that they say or do or suffer, is told us only to set Johnson in a clearer light. The unity of the picture is never broken. And that is the same thing as saying that Boswell is not merely what every one has seen, a unique collector of material : he is also what so few have seen, an artist of the very highest rank.

This is seen, too, in another important point. The danger of the hero-worshipping biographer is only too familiar to us. His book is usually a monotonous and insipid record of virtue or wisdom. The hero is always right, and always victorious, with the result that the book is at once tedious and incredible. But Boswell knew better than that. He was too much of an artist not to know that he wanted shadows to give value to his lights, and too much a lover of the fullness and variety of life not to want to get all of it that he possibly could into his picture. Like all great writers, there was scarcely anything he was afraid of handling, because there was scarcely anything of which he was not conscious that he could bend it to his will and force it to take its place, and no more than its place, in his scheme. Consequently, he has the courage to show us his hero, now wrong-headed and perverse, now rude almost to brutality, now so weak that the same resolution is repeated year after year only to be again broken and again renewed, now so gross and almost repulsive in his appearance and habits that it requires all his greatness to explain the welcome which well-bred men and refined women everywhere gave him. Nothing better shows the greatness of Boswell. He was not afraid to paint the wart on his Cromwell's nose, because he knew that he could so give the nobleness of the whole face, that the wart would merely add to the truthfulness of the portrait without detracting from its nobleness. The vast quantity of material which he brought into his book and the complete mastery which he maintained over it, is shown by the fact that few or no biographies record so many ridiculous or discreditable circumstances about their hero, and yet none leaves a more convincing impression of his greatness.

The notion, then, that the man who wrote the *Life of Johnson* was a fool, is an absurdity. If the arguments in its favour prove anybody a fool it is not Boswell. Nor is it even true that Boswell, like some great artists, escaped apparently by some divine gift from his natural folly just during the time necessary for the production of his great work, but at all other times relapsed at once into imbecility. We know how scrupulously accurate he was in what he wrote, not only from his candour in relating his own defeats, but from the many cases in which he confesses that he was not quite sure of the exact facts, such as, to give one instance, whether Johnson, on a certain occasion, spoke of " a page " or " ten lines " of Pope as not containing so much sense as one line of Cowley. Therefore we may take the picture he gives of himself in his book as a fair one. And what is it ? Does it bear out the notorious assertion that " there is not in all his books a single remark of his own on literature, politics, religion or society which is not either commonplace or absurd " ? One would sometimes imagine Macaulay had never read the book of which he speaks with such

E

confident decision. Certainly, except as a
biographer, Boswell was not a man of any
very remarkable abilities. But, in answer
to such an insult as Macaulay's, Boswell's
defenders may safely appeal to the book itself,
and to everybody who has read it with any
care. Will any one deny that not once or
twice, but again and again, the plain sense
of some subject which had been distorted
or confused by the perverse ingenuity of
Johnson " talking for victory " comes quietly,
after the smoke has cleared away, from the
despised imbecility of Boswell ? Who gives
the judgment which every one would now
give about the contest with the American
colonies ? Not Johnson but Boswell; not
the author of *Taxation No Tyranny*, but the
man who wrote so early as 1775 to his friend
Temple : " I am growing more and more an
American. I see the unreasonableness of
taxing them without the consent of their
Assemblies; I think our Ministry are mad in
undertaking this desperate war." Who was
right and who was wrong on the question of
the Middlesex Election ? Nobody now doubts
that Boswell was right, and Johnson was
wrong. Which has proved wiser, as we look
back, Johnson who ridiculed Gray's poetry,
or Boswell who sat up all night reading it ?
The fact is that Boswell was undoubtedly a

sensible and cultivated as well as a very
agreeable man, and as such was warmly
welcomed at the houses of the most intelligent
men of his day.

The old estimate, then, of James Boswell
must be definitely abandoned. The man who
knew him best, his friend Temple, the friend
of Gray, said of him that he was " the most
thinking man he had ever known " We may
not feel able to regard that as anything more
than the judgment of friendship : but it is
not fools who win such judgments even from
their friends. We may wonder at the word
" genius " being applied to him; and if genius
be taken in the stricter modern sense of
transcendent powers of mind, the sense in
which it is applied to Milton or Michael
Angelo, there is of course no doubt that it
would be absurd to apply it to Boswell. But
if the word be used in the old looser sense,
or if it be given the definite meaning of a man
who originates an important new departure
in a serious sphere of human action, who
creates something of a new order in art or
literature or politics or war, then Boswell's
claim to genius cannot be questioned. Just
as another member of Johnson's " Club " was
in those years writing history as it had never
been written before, so, and to a far more
remarkable degree, Boswell was writing

E 2

biography as it had never been written before. Gibbon's *Decline and Fall* was in fact a far less original performance, far less of a new departure, than Boswell's *Life of Johnson*. Boswell's book is in truth what he himself called it, "more of a life than any work that has ever yet appeared." After it the art of biography could never be merely what it had been before. And in that sense, the sense of a man whose work is an advance upon that of his predecessors, not merely in degree, but in kind, Boswell was undoubtedly and even more than Gibbon, entitled to the praise of genius.

Let us all, then, unashamedly and ungrudgingly give the rein to our admiration and love of Boswell. There is a hundred years between us and his follies, and every one of the hundred is full of his claim upon our gratitude. Let us now be ready to pay the debt in full. Let us be sure that there is something more than mere interest or entertainment in a book which so wise a man as Jowett confessed to having read fifty times, of which another lifelong thinker about life, a man very different from Jowett, Robert Louis Stevenson, could write: "I am taking a little Boswell daily by way of a Bible; I mean to read him now until the day I die." And not only in the book but in the author too. Let us be sure with Carlyle that if " Boswell wrote a good book " it was not because he was a fool, but on the contrary " because he had a heart and an eye to discern Wisdom, and an utterance to render it forth : because of his free insight, of his lively talent, above all of his love and childlike open-mindedness." In the particular business he had to carry through, these qualities were an equipment amounting to a modest kind of genius. They enabled him to produce a book which has given as much pleasure perhaps to intelligent men as any book that ever was written. Let us be careful whenever we think of Boswell to remember this side, the positive, creative, permanent side of him : and not so careful as our grandfathers generally were, to remember the other side which ceased to have any further importance on that night in May 1795 when he ended the fifty-five years of a life in which he had found time for more follies than most men, for more vices perhaps, certainly for more wisdom, but also for what most men never so much as conceive, the preparation and production of a masterpiece.

CHAPTER III

THE LIVES OF BOSWELL AND JOHNSON

THESE two men, then, are for ever insepar-able. They go down the centuries together, Johnson owing most of his immortality to the genius of Boswell, Boswell owing to Johnson that inspiring opportunity without which genius cannot discover that it is genius. There were other men in Johnson's circle, whom he knew longer and respected more: but for us, Boswell's position in relation to Johnson is unique. Beside him the others, even Burke and Reynolds, are, in this con-nection, shadows. They had their independ-ent fields of greatness in which Johnson had no share: Boswell's greatness is all John-sonian. We cannot think of him apart from Johnson: and he has so managed that we can scarcely think of Johnson apart from him. No one who occupies himself with the one can ignore the other: in interest and popularity they stand or fall together. It may be well, therefore, before going further, to give the bare facts of both their lives; dismissing Boswell first, as the less important, and then devoting the rest of the chapter to Johnson.

James Boswell was born in 1740. He came of an ancient family, a fact he never forgot, as, indeed, few people do who have the same advantage. His father was a Scottish judge with the title of Lord Auchinleck. The first of the family to hold the estate of Auchinleck, which is in Ayrshire, was Thomas Boswell, who received a grant of it from James IV in whose army he went to Flodden and shared the defeat and death of his patron. The estate had therefore belonged to the Boswells over two hundred years when the future biographer of Johnson was born. His father and he were never congenial spirits. The judge was a Whig with a practical view of life and had no sympathy with his son's romantic propensities either in religion, politics or literature. A plain Lowland Scot, he did not see why his son should take up with Toryism, Anglicanism, or literary hero-worship. When James, after first attaching himself to Paoli, the leader of the Corsican struggle for independence, returned home and took up the discipleship to Johnson which was to be the central fact in the rest of his life, his father frankly despaired of him, and broke out, according to Walter Scott: "There's nae hope for Jamie, mon. Jamie is gaen clean gyte. What do you think, mon ? He's done wi' Paoli—he's off wi' the landlouping scoundrel of a Corsican; and whose tail do you think he has pinned himself to now, mon ? A *dominie*, mon—an auld dominie : he keeped a schule, and cau'd it an acaadamy." Well might Boswell say that they were " so totally different that a good understanding is scarcely possible." Beside disliking Paoli and Johnson, Lord Auchinleck cared nothing for some of Boswell's strict feudal notions, had the bad taste to give his son a step-mother, and to be as unlike him as possible in the matter of good spirits. Scarcely anything could interfere with the judge's cheerfulness, while Boswell was always falling into depressions about nothing in particular and perhaps indulging in the " foolish notion," rebuked by Johnson, that " melancholy is a proof of acuteness." But in spite of their differences the father and son managed to avoid anything like a definite breach. Boswell was sincerely anxious to please his father, and was constantly urged in that direction by his great mentor : and after all the judge went some way to meet his singular son, for he paid his debts and entertained both Paoli and Johnson at Auchinleck. The latter visit was naturally a source of some anxiety to Boswell and it did not go off without a storm when the old Whig and the old Tory unluckily got on to the topic of Charles I and Cromwell : but all ended well, and Boswell characteristically ends his story of it, written after both were dead, with the pious hope that the antagonists had by then met in a higher state of existence " where there is no room for Whiggism."

Full of activities as Boswell's life was, the definite facts and dates in it are not very numerous. He was sent to Glasgow University, and wished to be a soldier, but was bred by his father to the law. No doubt he gave some early signs of intellectual promise, for which it was not thought the army provided a fit sphere, for the Duke of Argyle is reported to have said to his father when he was only twenty : " My lord, I like your son : this boy must not be shot at for three-and-sixpence a day." He paid his first visit to London in 1760; and, having heard a good deal about Johnson from one Mr. Gentleman, and from Derrick, a very minor poet, he at once sought an introduction, but had to leave London without succeeding in his object. He was equally unsuccessful when he was in London the next year, during which he published some anonymous poems which would not have helped him to secure the desired introduction. The great event occurred at last in 1763. The day was the 16th of May and the scene the house of Davies, the bookseller. "At last," says Boswell, "on

Monday the 16th of May, when I was sitting in Mr. Davies's back-parlour, after having drunk tea with him and Mrs. Davies, Johnson unexpectedly came into the shop ; and Mr. Davies having perceived him through the glass-door in the room in which we were sitting, advancing towards us,—he announced his aweful approach to me, somewhat in the manner of an actor in the part of Horatio, when he addresses Hamlet on the appearance of his father's ghost, 'Look, my Lord, it comes.' "

So, with characteristic accuracy and characteristic imagination, begins his well-known account of his first meeting with his hero, and the storms to which he was exposed in its course. But all ended satisfactorily, for when the great man was gone, Davies reassured the nervous Boswell by saying: "Don't be uneasy, I can see he likes you very well." A few days afterwards Boswell called on Johnson at his Chambers in the Temple, and the great friendship which was the pleasure and business of his life was definitely begun. Yet it is worth remembering, if only as an additional proof of Boswell's biographical genius, that, according to the calculation of Dr. Birkbeck Hill, when all the weeks and months during which Johnson and Boswell were living within reach of each other are added together, they amount to little more than two years. And of course this includes all the days on which they were both in London, on many, or rather most, of which they did not meet.

A few months after the first meeting, Boswell went by his father's wish to Utrecht to study law. But before that the friendship was got on to a firm footing, and Boswell had had the pride and pleasure of hearing Johnson say, " There are few people whom I take so much to, as you." A still stronger proof of Johnson's feeling was that he insisted on going with Boswell to Harwich to see him out of England. This was the occasion on which he scarified the good Protestants who were with them in the coach by defending the Inquisition, and invited one of the ladies who said she never allowed her children to be idle to take his own education in hand; "'for I have been an idle fellow all my life.' 'I am sure, sir,' said she, 'you have not been idle.' 'Nay, madam, it is very true, and that gentleman there,' pointing to me, 'has been idle. He was idle at Edinburgh. His father sent him to Glasgow where he continued to be idle. He then came to London where he has been very idle; and now he is going to Utrecht where he will be as idle as ever.' I asked him privately how he could expose me so. 'Pooh, Pooh!' said he, 'they know nothing about you and will think of it no more.'" When he was not engaged in these alarums and excursions or in reproving Boswell for giving the coachman a shilling instead of the customary sixpence, he was occupied in reading Pomponius Mela *De Situ Orbis*. How complete the picture is and how vivid! It once more gives Boswell's method in miniature.

He seems to have stayed at Utrecht about a year, afterwards travelling in Germany, where he visited Wittenberg, and sat down to write to Johnson in the church where the Reformation was first preached, with his paper resting on the tomb of Melanchthon. It is noticeable that, though he had only known Johnson a year, he already hoped to be his biographer. "At this tomb, then, my ever dear and respected friend, I vow to thee an eternal attachment. It shall be my study to do what I can to render your life happy: and, if you die before me, I shall endeavour to do honour to your memory." He was also at this time in Italy and Switzerland, where he visited Voltaire and gratified him by quoting a remark of Johnson's that Frederick the Great's writings were the sort of stuff one might expect from " a footboy who had been Voltaire's amanuensis." Nor did this collector of celebrities omit to visit Rousseau, the rival lion of the day, between whom and Voltaire the orthodox Johnson thought it was " difficult to settle the proportion of iniquity." But as far as Boswell's records go, he never said such violent things of Voltaire as of Rousseau, whom he called " a rascal who ought to be hunted out of society and transported to work in the plantations." Boswell, however, was an admirer of the *Vicaire Savoyard*, and said what he could in defence of his host, in return for the hospitality he had enjoyed at Neuchâtel, with the usual result, of course, that Johnson only became more outrageous.

In 1765 Boswell made the acquaintance of another distinguished man with whom his name will always be connected. Corsica had at that time been long, and on the whole victoriously, engaged in a struggle to free itself from the hated rule of Genoa. The leader of the Corsicans was a man of high birth, character and abilities, Pascal Paoli, who had acted since 1753 at once as their General and as the head of the civil administration. Both the generous and the curious element in Boswell made him anxious not to return from Italy without seeing something of so interesting a people and so great a hero. Armed with introductions from Rousseau and others and with such protection as a British Captain's letter could give him against Barbary Corsairs, he sailed from Leghorn to Corsica in September 1765. His account of the island and of his tour there, published in 1768, is still very good reading. He soon made his way to the palace where Paoli was residing, with whom he at first felt himself in a presence more awe-inspiring than that of princes, but ventured after a while upon a compliment to the Corsicans. " Sir, I am upon my travels, and have lately visited Rome. I am come from seeing the ruins of one brave and free people : I now see the rise of another." The good sense of Paoli declined any parallel between Rome and his own little people, but he soon received Boswell into his intimacy and spent some hours alone with him almost every day. One fine answer of his, uniting the scholar and the patriot, is worth quoting. Boswell asked him how he, who confessed to his love of society and particularly of the society of learned and cultivated men, could be content to pass his life in an island where no such advantages were to be had; to which Paoli replied at once—

" Vincit amor patriæ laudumque immensa cupido."

Well might Boswell wish to have a statue of him taken at that moment. Even Virgilian quotation has seldom been put to nobler use. Like all the great men of the eighteenth century, Paoli was an enthusiast for the ancients. "A young man who would form his mind to glory," he told Boswell, "must not read modern memoirs; *ma Plutarcho, ma Tito Livio.*" His own mind was formed not only to glory, but also to what so often fails to go with glory, to justice and moderation. Nothing is more remarkable in the conversations with him recorded by Boswell than his good sense and fairness of mind in speaking of the Genoese. Even in the excitement of Corsica, Boswell did not forget Johnson. He says that he quoted specimens of Johnson's wisdom to Paoli, who "translated them to the Corsican heroes with Italian energy"; and, as he had written to his master "from the tomb of Melanchthon sacred to learning and piety," so he also wrote to him "from the palace of Pascal Paoli sacred to wisdom and liberty." Boswell was received with great honour in Corsica, no doubt partly because he was very naturally supposed to have some mission from the British Government. He left the island in December and arrived in London in February 1766, when his intimacy with Johnson was at once resumed, in spite

of the visits to Rousseau and Voltaire which
drew some inevitable sarcasms from the great
man. He soon, however, returned to Scotland, where he was admitted an Advocate in
the summer of 1766.

Johnson thought he was too busy about
Corsica, and wrote to him: "Empty your
head of Corsica, which I think has filled it
rather too long." But this was in March
1768, when Boswell's *Account of Corsica* had
already been published. It sold very well,
a second and a third edition appearing within
the year. Gray and other good judges spoke
warmly of it and it seems that a French
translation as well as two Dutch ones were
made. It caused so much stir and aroused so
much sympathy in England that Lord Holland
was quite afraid we were going to be "so
foolish as to go to war because Mr. Boswell
has been in Corsica." After this it was less
likely than ever that Boswell would forget
that island. Motives of vanity combined with
his genuine enthusiasm to keep him full of it,
and he replied to Johnson's monition:
"Empty my head of Corsica! empty it of
honour, empty it of humanity, empty it of
friendship, empty it of piety! No! while
I live, Corsica and the cause of the brave
islanders shall ever employ much of my
attention and interest me in the sincerest

manner." It seems from his letters to Temple
that he found these outbursts a great deal
easier than living in a manner worthy of a
friend of Paoli. But he did more than talk.
He wrote to Chatham to try to interest him
in Corsica, and received a reply three pages
long applauding his generous warmth; he
brought out a volume of *British Essays in
Favour of the Brave Corsicans*, sent Paoli
Johnson's Works and, what was more substantial, forwarded a quantity of ordnance,
to buy which he had managed to raise a
subscription of £700. His desire to be a well-
known man now began to receive some gratifi-
cation and he frankly confesses his pleasure
at having such men as Johnson, Hume and
Franklin dining with him at his chambers.
Nor will any reasonable man blame him.
His snobbishness, if it is to be so called, was
always primarily a snobbishness of mind and
character, not of wealth or rank.

Nothing else of importance occurred to him
in these years. He was much occupied with
the great law-suit about the succession to the
Douglas property, on which he wrote two
pamphlets and was so sure of the justice of his
view that he once dared to tell Johnson he
knew nothing about that subject. He was
with Johnson at Oxford in 1768 and they
were already talking of going to the Hebrides

F

together. The next year, 1769, saw the conquest of Corsica by the French to whom the Genoese had ceded their claims. The result was that Paoli came to London, where he lived till 1789, and Boswell was constantly with him. In this year he did at least one very foolish thing, and at least one very wise one. He made himself ridiculous by going to the Shakespeare Jubilee at Stratford and appearing in Corsican costume with " *Viva la Libertà* " embroidered on his cap. He also took the most sensible step of his whole life in marrying his cousin, Margaret Montgomerie, on November 25. She never liked Johnson, and her husband had the candour to report an excellent sally of hers at his and his sage's expense : " I have seen many a bear led by a man; but I never before saw a man led by a bear." But though, as Boswell says, she could not be expected to like his " irregular hours and uncouth habits," she never failed in courtesy to him : and he on his part was unwearied in sending friendly messages to his " dear enemy " as he called her, and was well aware of her importance to her husband. The event unhappily proved his prescience; for after her death in 1789, Boswell's downward course was visibly accelerated.

After Boswell's marriage there was no

communication between him and Johnson for a year and a half, and they did not meet again till March 1772, when Boswell came to London, and stayed some time. The next year he came again, and, by Johnson's active support, was elected a member of " The Club," a small society of friends founded by Reynolds and Johnson in 1764. At first it met weekly for supper, but after a few years the members began the custom of dining together on fixed dates which has continued to the present day. Among the members when Boswell was elected were Johnson and Reynolds, Burke, Goldsmith and Garrick. Gibbon and Charles Fox came in the next year, and Adam Smith in 1775. In 1780 the number of members was enlarged to thirty-five which is still the limit. "The Club" has always maintained its distinction, and a recent article in the *Edinburgh Review* records that fifteen Prime Ministers have been members of it, as well as men like Scott, Tennyson, Hallam, Macaulay and Grote. The first advantage over and above pride and pleasure derived by Boswell from his election was the acquaintance of Burke, which he had long desired and retained through life. Burke said of him that he had so much good humour naturally that it was scarcely a virtue in him.

In the autumn of that year, 1773, Johnson

and Boswell made their famous tour to the Hebrides. They, in fact, went over much more than the Hebrides, seeing the four Universities of Edinburgh, St. Andrews, Aberdeen and Glasgow, besides many less famous places. Johnson says they were everywhere "received like princes in their progress," and though no doubt hospitality was freer in those days when travellers were few and inns poor, yet the whole story is a remarkable proof of Johnson's fame and Boswell's popularity. The University Professors vied with each other in paying civilities to Johnson, the town of Aberdeen gave him its freedom, and among their hosts were magnates like the Duke of Argyll, Lord Errol and Lord Loudoun, who " jumped for joy " at their coming, and great men of law or learning like Lord Monboddo and Lord Elibank.

By this time all the important events in Boswell's life were over except the publication of his two great books, the *Tour to the Hebrides* and the *Life of Johnson*. During all the ten years which Johnson still had to live, except 1780 and 1782, the two friends managed to spend some time together, and when they did not, the friendship was maintained by correspondence. Boswell's father died in 1782, and Boswell came into possession of the estate, worth £1,600 a year. Johnson and Boswell took more than one " jaunt " in the country together, visiting Oxford, Lichfield and other places. They were at Oxford together in June 1784; but Johnson was then evidently failing. On their return to London, Boswell busied himself with the help of Reynolds in trying to get Johnson's pension increased, so that he might be able to spend the winter abroad. Johnson was very pleased on hearing of the attempt, saying, when Boswell told him, "'This is taking prodigious pains about a man.' 'O, sir,' said Boswell, 'your friends would do everything for you.' He paused, grew more and more agitated, till tears started into his eyes, and he exclaimed with fervent emotion, 'God bless you all.' I was so affected that I also shed tears. After a short silence he renewed and extended his grateful benediction, 'God bless you all, for Jesus Christ's sake.'" Those were the last words Boswell heard under Johnson's roof. The next day they both dined with Reynolds, and on July 2 Boswell left London, to see Johnson no more. Johnson died on the 13th of December 1784.

Fitful and unsuccessful legal and political ambitions occupied a large part of Boswell's later years. He made some approaches to standing as a candidate for Ayrshire in 1784,

and again in 1788, was called to the English
Bar in 1786, attached himself to Lord Lonsdale,
and hoped to enter Parliament for one of his
boroughs, but seems to have got nothing out
of his connection with that insolent old bully
but a certain amount of humiliation and the
Recordership of Carlisle. That unimportant
office was the only substantial reward he
received from all his long suit and service in
the antechambers of law and politics. Whatever he achieved he owed to literature and the
friends his love of literature had brought him.
It was not the laird or the lawyer, but the
friend and biographer of Johnson whom
the Royal Academy appointed in 1791 to
the complimentary office of their Secretary
for Foreign Correspondence. And those last
years, while they brought him disappoint-
ment in everything else, saw him take definite
rank as a successful author. The *Tour to the
Hebrides* was published in 1785, and sold out
in a few weeks. The third edition was issued
within a year of the appearance of the first.
It was followed by the publication of Johnson's
famous Letter to Lord Chesterfield and of an
account of his Conversation with George III,
and finally in 1791 by the *Life* itself. A
second edition of this was called for in 1793.
Boswell only lived two years more. He died
on May 19, 1795. He left two sons: Alexander,

who became Sir Alexander, was the principal mover in the matter of the Burns Monument on the banks of Doon, and was killed in a duel in 1822; and James, who supplied notes for the third edition of his father's great book, and edited the third *Variorum Shakespeare*, known as Boswell's *Malone*, in 1821.

Such were the main outlines of the life of the biographer. We may now turn to those of the life which he owes his fame to recording. They are in most ways very unlike his own. Samuel Johnson was very far from being heir to a large estate and an ancient name. He was the son of a bookseller at Lichfield, and was born there on the 18th of September 1709, in a house which is now preserved in public hands in memory of the event of that day. His father's family was so obscure that he once said, " I can hardly tell who was my grandfather." His mother was Sarah Ford, who came of a good yeoman stock in Warwickshire. She was both a good and an intelligent woman. Samuel was the elder and only ultimately surviving issue of the marriage. A picturesque incident in his childhood is that his mother took him to London to be " touched " by Queen Anne for the scrofula, or " king's evil," as it was called, from which he suffered. He must have been one of the last persons to go through this curious ceremony, which the Georges never performed, though the service for it remained in the Book of Common Prayer for some years after the accession of George I. The boy made an impression upon people from the first. He liked to recall in later life that the dame who first taught him to read brought him a present of gingerbread when he was starting for Oxford, and told him he was the best scholar she had ever had. Afterwards he went to Lichfield School, and at the age of fifteen to Stourbridge. At both he was evidently held in respect by boys and masters alike. Probably the curious combination in him of the invalid and the prize-fighter which was conspicuous all through his life, already arrested attention in his boyhood. He played none of the ordinary games, but yet, as we have already seen, was acknowledged as a leader by the boys, and his abilities were the pride of the school. He already exhibited the amazing memory which enabled him in later life to dictate to Boswell his famous letter to Chesterfield rather than search for a copy, and to confute a person who praised a bad translation from Martial by a contemptuous " Why, sir, the original is thus," followed by a recitation not only of the Latin original which it is not likely he had looked at for years, but also of the translation which he had only read once. So on another occasion when Baretti, who had read a little Ariosto with him some years before, proposed to give him some more lessons, but feared he might have forgotten their previous readings, " Who forgets, sir ? " said Johnson, and immediately repeated three or four stanzas of the *Orlando*. To the lover of literature there is no possession more precious than a good verbal memory, and this Johnson enjoyed to a very unusual degree all through his life. But it is worth noting that he was entirely free from the defect which commonly results from an exceptional memory. He always thought and spoke for himself, and was never prevented from using his own mind and his own words by the fact that his memory supplied him abundantly with those of others. His scholarly friend Langton annoyed him by depending upon books too much in his conversation, and one of his compliments to Boswell was, " You and I do not talk from books."

After he left Stourbridge he spent two years at home in desultory reading, " not voyages and travels, but all literature, sir, all ancient writers, all manly; though but little Greek, only some of Anacreon and Hesiod," the result of which was that when he went up to Oxford, the Master of his College said he was " the best qualified for the University that he had ever known come there." His College was Pembroke, of which he became a Commoner (not a Servitor, as Carlyle said) in 1728. The Oxford of that day was not a place of much discipline and the official order of study was very laxly maintained. It seems not to have meant much to Johnson, and he is described as having spent a good deal of his time "lounging at the College gates with a circle of young students round him, whom he was entertaining with wit and keeping from their studies." Most good talkers find the first real sphere for their talent when they get to the University, and the best of all was not likely to be an exception, nor to resist that strongest of the intellectual temptations. But he did some solid reading, especially Greek, though he seemed to himself to be very idle, perhaps because his standard was so high that he used to say in later life, "I never knew a man who studied hard." So when he confesses the imperfections of his Greek scholarship, and other people exaggerate his confession, it is well to remember the reply made by Jacob Bryant when Gifford in an argument quoted Johnson's admission that "he was not a good Greek scholar," "Sir, it is not easy for us to say what such a man as Johnson would call a good Greek scholar." A man whose remedy for sleeplessness was to turn Greek epigrams into Latin was at any rate not ignorant of Greek.

Johnson was prevented by his poverty from getting the full advantages either out of the life or the studies of Oxford. His want of shoes prevented his attending lectures, his pride forbad him to receive doles of help, the friend, said to be a Mr. Corbet of Shropshire, on whose promises of support he had relied in going to Oxford, failed him, his father's business went from little to less; with the inevitable result that he had to leave Oxford without a degree. This was in December 1729. But he had made an impression there, had a strong affection for his College, and liked going to stay there in the days of his glory. His usual host was one Dr. Adams, the Master of Pembroke, who had once been his tutor but told Boswell that the relation was only nominal; "he was above my mark." When he left Oxford he returned to his Lichfield home, where his father died two months later, leaving so little behind him that all that Johnson received of his estate was twenty pounds. He seems to have remained at Lichfield, where the poverty of his family did not prevent his mixing with the most cultivated society of a town rich in cultivated people, till 1732, when he became an usher in a school at Market Bosworth. He hated this monotonous drudgery and left it after a few months, going to live with a Mr. Warren, the first bookseller to establish himself at Birmingham, whom he helped by his knowledge of literature. While in Birmingham he did a translation of a Jesuit book about Abyssinia, for which Warren paid him five guineas. In 1734 he returned to Lichfield, tried without success to obtain subscribers for an edition of the poems of Politian, and offered to write in the *Gentleman's Magazine*. It is difficult to see how he supported himself at this period : perhaps he was helped by his mother or by his brother who carried on the bookselling business till his death a little later. Anyhow it was just at this time that he took a step for which poverty generally finds the courage more quickly than wealth. He married Elizabeth Porter at St. Werburgh's Church, Derby, in July 1735. Mrs. Porter was a widow twice his age and not of an attractive appearance; but there is no doubt that Johnson's love for her was sincere and lasting. To the end of his life he remembered her frequently in his prayers " if it were lawful," and kept the anniversary of her death with prayers and tears. Eighteen years after she died he could write in his private note-books that his grief for her was not abated and that he had less pleasure in any good that happened to him, because she could not share it : and in 1782 when she had been dead thirty years, and he was drawing near his own end, he prays for her and after doing so, noted " perhaps Tetty knows that I prayed for her. Perhaps Tetty is now praying for me. God help me."

This was the inner truth of the relation between Johnson and his elderly wife, but it was natural and indeed inevitable that the world, the little world of their acquaintances, should have been chiefly alive to the humorous external aspect of the marriage, and one does not wonder that his friend Beauclerk, who had been through the divorce court, should have enjoyed relating that Johnson had said to him, " Sir, it was a love marriage on both sides ! " Johnson's own account of the actual wedding is singular enough. " Sir, she had read the old romances, and had got into her head the fantastical notion that a woman of spirit should use her lover like a dog. So, sir, at first she told me that I rode too fast, and she could not keep up with me ; and, when I rode a little slower, she passed me, and complained that I lagged behind. I was not to be made the slave of caprice ; and I resolved to begin as I meant to end. I therefore pushed on briskly, till I was fairly out of her sight. The road lay between two hedges, so I was sure she could not miss it ; and I contrived that she should soon come up with me. When she did, I observed her to be in tears."

Mrs. Johnson was the widow of a Birmingham draper, and brought her husband several hundred pounds, part of which was at once spent in hiring and furnishing a large house at Edial near Lichfield where Johnson proposed to take pupils. But no pupils came except David Garrick and his brother, the sons of an old Lichfield friend, and the " academy " was abandoned after a year and a half. The lack of pupils, however, was perhaps a blessing in disguise, for it enabled Johnson to write most of his tragedy *Irene*, with which he went to London in March 1737. His pupil, David Garrick, went with him to study law, and when Garrick was a rich, famous and rather vain man, Johnson, who liked to curb the "insolence of wealth " once referred to 1737 as the year " when I came to London with twopence halfpenny in my pocket; and thou, Davy, with three-halfpence in thine." Nothing came of this first visit to the capital. He lived as best he could, dining for eightpence, and seeing a few friends, one of whom was Henry Hervey, son of the Earl of Bristol, of whose kindness he always retained an affectionate memory, so that he once said to Boswell, " If you call a dog Hervey, I shall love him." In the summer he returned to Lichfield, and finished his tragedy, after which he brought his wife back with him to London which was his home for the rest of his life. Efforts to get *Irene* performed were unsuccessful, but he soon began to write regularly for the *Gentleman's Magazine*, of which he held so high an opinion that he looked " with reverence " on the house where it was printed. To this he contributed essays and was soon employed to write the *Parliamentary Debates* which, in the days before reporters, were made up with fictitious names from such scanty notes as could be got of the actual speeches. There is a story of his being, many years later, in a company who were praising a famous oration of Chatham, and were naturally a good deal startled by his quietly saying, " That speech I wrote in a garret in Exeter Street." He continued to do this work till 1743 when he became aware that the speeches were taken as authentic and refused to be " accessory to the propagation of falsehood." But, while engaged in it, he had had no scruples about taking care " that the Whig dogs should not have the best of it."

A much more important matter than this hack-work was the publication of his *London*, a poem in imitation of the Third Satire of Juvenal. This appeared in May 1738. He got ten guineas for it, which he was in no position to despise; but he also got something much more important, an established name in the world of letters. Every one talked of him, and Pope, who published his " 1738 " in the same year, was not only generous enough to inquire about him, and to say when told that the author of *London* was some obscure man, " He will soon be *déterré*," but also to try to get him an Irish degree of M.A. This was in view of some attempts Johnson made to escape from dependence on journalism for his daily bread : but they were all unsuccessful, and till he received his pension his only source of income was what his various writings produced. In such circumstances he naturally wrote many things of quite ephemeral interest which call for no mention now. Perhaps the only prose work of permanent value he produced in these years was the life of his mysterious friend, Richard Savage. This curious volume appeared in 1744. The subject of it died in 1743. He and Johnson had been companions both in extreme poverty and in the intellectual pleasures which in such men poverty is unable to annihilate. Mrs. Johnson seems to have been out of London at this time, and the two struggling men of letters often passed nights together, walking and talking in the streets and squares without the price of a night's lodging between them. Johnson's account of his friend did not fill his pocket, but must have contributed something to his fame as it was very favourably criticized. It was the occasion of Reynolds first becoming acquainted with his name. He was so interested by the book that, having taken it up while standing with his arm leaning upon a chimney-piece, he read the whole without sitting down and found his arm quite benumbed when he got to the end.

" Slow rises worth by poverty depressed." Johnson had now been seven years in London, but had not yet found the way to do anything worthy of his powers. If he had died then, only the curious and the learned would have known his name to-day. A single satire in verse would never, by itself, have had the force to push its way through the ever-increasing crowd of applicants that besiege the attention of posterity. But the next year, 1745, is the literary turning-point of his life. Before it was over he had begun to deal with two subjects with which much of his remaining life was occupied, and on which much of his fame depends. He had published a pamphlet upon Shakespeare's *Macbeth* which won the praise of Warburton, for which Johnson always felt and showed his gratitude (" He praised me at a time when praise was of value to me "); and, if Boswell is right, he had begun to occupy

G

himself with the idea of making an English Dictionary. Thus, poor and obscure as he was in those years, sick with deferred hope as he must have been, he had in fact laid the foundation-stones of the authority and fame he was soon to enjoy as the Editor of Shakespeare and above all as " Dictionary Johnson." Now at last he began to do work worthier of his powers. The " *Plan for a Dictionary of the English Language* " was published in 1747 and in the same year he wrote the admirable *Prologue* for the opening of Drury Lane Theatre, of which his pupil, David Garrick, more fortunate than the master with whom he had come to London, was now become manager.

Two years later Garrick produced the long-delayed tragedy of *Irene*. It is not a great drama, as Johnson well knew, at least in his later years. There is a story of his being told that a certain Mr. Pot called it " the finest tragedy of modern times," to which his only reply was, " If Pot says so, Pot lies." But this hardly has the genuine ring about it. Even Garrick's talent and friendship could not make *Irene* a success, but the performance brought Johnson a little welcome profit and enabled him to sell the book to Dodsley for a hundred pounds. In the same year, 1749, a more lasting evidence of his poetic powers was given by the appearance of *The Vanity of Human Wishes*, another Juvenalian imitation, but freer and bolder than the first. From 1750 to 1752 he was writing *The Rambler*, a sort of newspaper essay which appeared every Tuesday and Friday. He wrote it almost entirely himself, and almost always at the last moment, when the printer was calling for it. No one will now wonder that it never had a large circulation as a periodical, for it usually exhibits him at his gravest, and many of the essays are scarcely distinguishable from sermons. But that age had grave tastes and few temptations to intellectual frivolity. We have seen that the idlest sort of reading Johnson could think of for a boy was " voyages and travels "; novels he does not mention, indeed there were then very few of them; plays he rather strangely ignores : newspapers, as we now know them and suffer by them, he of course could not so much as conceive. *The Rambler* had no sixpenny magazines of triviality, no sensational halfpenny papers, to compete with it, and it pursued an even course of modest success for its two years of life. The greatest pleasure it brought Johnson was the praise of his wife, who said to him, " I thought very well of you before ; but I did not imagine you could have written anything equal to this." That was just the discovery a good

G 2

many people beside his wife were making about Johnson in those years : with the result that when *The Rambler* appeared as a book, it sold well and had gone through twelve editions by the time Boswell wrote its author's life.

Three years after the cessation of *The Rambler* and, unhappily, also three years after the death of his wife, with whom it would have been his chief happiness to share his success, the great Dictionary appeared. It may safely be said that no single Englishman has ever accomplished a literary task of such vast extent. The mere labour, one might say the mere dull drudgery, of collecting and arranging the materials of such a work is enormous. Nor could any literary labour bring with it greater temptations. Johnson's success is not more due to his learning and powers of mind than to the good sense which never failed him and the strong will which he could generally exert when he chose. He pleased himself at first, as he tells us in his Preface, " with a prospect of the hours which I should revel away in feasts of literature "; but that, of course, was where the danger lay. A man of an equally strong love of literature and a weaker will would have allowed himself to be swept away by the indulgence of curiosity, and the luxury of desultory reading; but Johnson soon saw

that these visions of intellectual pleasure were
" the dreams of a poet doomed at last to wake
a lexicographer "; and that, if he was to do
the thing he had undertaken to do, he must
set stern limits, not only to the pleasures of
study, but also to the delusive quest of unattainable perfection, which is the constant
parent of futility. He realized, as so many
men of letters have failed to realize, that " to
deliberate whenever I doubted, to inquire
whenever I was ignorant, would have pro-
tracted the undertaking without end and
perhaps without much improvement "; and
instead of attempting the impossible and
achieving nothing, he was wise enough and
modest enough, by attempting only the
attainable, to place himself in a position to
achieve all that he attempted.

The praise he deserved was somewhat slow
in coming, as is commonly the case with the
greatest literary achievements. But though,
as he sadly says in the last words of his great
Preface, most of those whom he wished to
please had sunk into the grave, and he had
therefore little to hope or fear from praise or
censure, yet he was always and before all
things a human being, and only a creature
above or below humanity could have been
insensible to the pleasure of the new fame, the
new authority and the new friends which his

Dictionary gradually brought him. Before many years had passed the " harmless drudge," as he himself had defined a lexicographer, had become the acknowledged law-giver and dicta- tor of English letters; he had gathered round him a society of the finest minds of that generation, he had received a public pension which secured his independence, he had begun the long friendship which gave him a second home for more than fifteen years. These things did not all come at once—he did not know the Thrales till 1764 or 1765—but the true turning-point in his career is the publica- tion of his Dictionary. He was still poor for some years after that, and still much occupied in the production of hack-work : but he was never again obscure and was soon to be famous. Within a year after the appearance of the Dictionary he had issued his *Proposals for an Edition of Shakespeare*, the second in time and perhaps in importance of his three great works. His new position secured him a good number of subscribers and he in- tended to publish it the next year, 1757; but the interruptions of indolence, business and pleasure, as he himself says of Pope, usually disappoint the sanguine expectations of authors, and the book did not in fact appear till 1765.

Neither Shakespeare nor idleness had occupied the whole of the intervening years. From 1758 to 1760 he produced a weekly paper called *The Idler*, of the same character as *The Rambler*. In 1759 he wrote his once famous story *Rasselas* to pay the expenses of his mother's funeral. It was written in the evenings of a single week. Good judges thought that, if he had known how to make a bargain, he ought to have received as much as four hundred pounds for this book, which was translated into most of the European languages; but he did not in fact receive more than a hundred pounds for the first and twenty-five for the second edition. By this time he could visit Oxford, from which University he had received the degree of M.A. when his Dictionary was on the eve of publication : and another sign of the position he was beginning to occupy is that we find Smollet writing of him in 1759 as the " great Cham of literature." More substantial evidences followed in 1762 when George III was advised by Bute to grant him a pension of £300 a year, an income which must have seemed boundless affluence to a man who had never known a time when five pounds was not an important sum to him.

Next year came the event which was even more important to his fame than the receipt of the pension was to his comfort. In 1763 he met Boswell for the first time. Fortune now began to smile upon him in good earnest and evidences of his established position and prosperity follow each other in rapid succession. "The Club" (its proper and still existing name, though Boswell occasionally calls it The Literary Club) was founded in 1764 and provided him for the rest of his life with an ideal theatre for the display of his amazing powers of talk, though it appears that he was not in his later years a very regular attendant. The next year, 1765, was probably the year in which he first met Thrale, the great brewer, and his clever and ambitious wife. No event contributed so much to the happiness of his after years. Thrale was a man of character and understanding, and was not without scholarly tastes. He at once saw the value of such a friend as Johnson, lived in the closest intimacy with him for the rest of his days, and named him executor in his will, which gave Johnson an opportunity such as he always liked, of mixing in business, and incidentally also, of saying the best thing that ever was said at the sale of a brewery. He appeared at the auction, according to the story told by Lord Lucan, "bustling about with an inkhorn and pen in his button-hole, like an excise-man; and, on being asked what he really considered to be the value of the

property, answered, ' We are not here to sell
a parcel of boilers and vats, but the poten-
tiality of growing rich beyond the dreams of
avarice.' " The brewery was sold for £135,000
to Mr. Barclay, the founder of the present firm
of Barclay & Perkins, who now put Johnson's
head on the labels of their beer bottles. But
it was not so much on the silent and busy
Thrale himself as on his wife, a quick and
clever woman fond of literary society, that
the visible burden, honour and pleasure of
the long friendship with Johnson fell. Till
the breach caused by her second marriage
just before he died no one had so much
of his society as Mrs. Thrale. She soon
became " my mistress " to him, an adaptation
of his from the " my master " which was her
phrase for her husband. And for him, too,
Thrale was " my master." A somewhat
masterful servant, no doubt, to them both,
but he loved them sincerely and was deeply
grateful for their kindness. He lived at their
house at Streatham as much as he liked, and
had his own room reserved for him both there
and at their London house. At Streatham he
sometimes remained for several months, and
it is chiefly there that Boswell's only rival,
Fanny Burney, saw him. It may be said that
the Thrales' house was more of a home to him
than anything else he ever knew : it was at

least the only house since his childhood in
which he ever lived with children. There in
the garden or in the library he studied and
idled and talked at his ease; there many of his
friends gathered round him; there his wishes
were anticipated and his words listened to,
sometimes with fear, sometimes with amusement, sometimes with reverence, always with
affection and almost always with admiration.
Well might he write to Mrs. Thrale as he did
in October 1777 : " I cannot but think on your
kindness and my master's. Life has upon the
whole fallen short, very short, of my early
expectation; but the acquisition of such a
friendship, at an age when new friendships are
seldom acquired, is something better than the
general course of things gives man a right to
expect. I think on it with great delight. I
am not very apt to be delighted."

Johnson had now become a comparatively
prosperous man, and the lives of the prosperous have a way of producing little to record.
He received many honours and compliments
of different sorts. Dublin University made
him LL.D. in 1765, he had his well-known
interview with George III in 1767, the Royal
Academy appointed him their Professor in
Ancient Literature in 1769, and in 1775 he
received the honorary degree of D.C.L. from
the University of Oxford. But the only events

of any special importance in the last twenty
years of his life were the publication of his
Shakespeare in 1765, his journey in Scotland
with Boswell in 1773, and the writing of his
last and most popular book, *The Lives of the
Poets*. This he undertook in 1777 and com-
pleted in 1781. Its easier style, pleasant
digressions, and occasional bits of autobiography, represent the change that had come
over Johnson's life. He was now a man at
ease and wrote like one. For the note of
disappointed youthful ambition which is only
half concealed in the earlier works it sub-
stitutes an old man's kindliness of retrospect.
Matters of less importance in these years were
the publication of his *Journey to the Western
Islands*, of the *Prologue* to Goldsmith's *Good-
Natured Man* and of his political pamphlets,
The False Alarm, *Falkland's Islands*, *The
Patriot*, and *Taxation no Tyranny*. But none
of these things except the *Lives of the Poets*
occupied much of his time, and his principal
occupation in his old age was talking to his
friends. He travelled a good deal, often
visiting Oxford, his old home at Lichfield,
and his friend Taylor's house in Derbyshire.
In 1775 he went to France with the Thrales,
and even in his last year was planning a tour
to Italy. But by that time the motive was
rather health than pleasure. He had a

paralytic stroke in 1783 and lost his powers of speech for some days. One of the doctors who attended him was Dr. Heberden, who had cured Cowper of a still graver illness twenty years earlier. His strong constitution enabled him to recover rapidly, and within a month he was paying visits in Kent and Wiltshire. But he had other complaints, and never again knew even that modest measure of health which he had once enjoyed.

The inevitable loss of friends, that saddest and most universal sorrow of old age, joined with illness to depress his last years. Beauclerk died in 1780, Thrale in 1781, Levett and Mrs. Williams, two of the humble friends to whom his charity had given a home in his house, in 1782 and 1783. He was left almost alone. Yet the old courage and love of society asserted itself to the last, and he founded a new dining club the year before he died. But it was too late. The year 1784 opened with a prolonged illness lasting for months, and though in the summer he was well enough to get away to Oxford with Boswell once more, all could see that the end could not be far off. It came on the 13th of December 1784. He was buried in Westminster Abbey on December 20th. Burke and Windham, with Colman the dramatist and Sir Joseph Bankes the President of the Royal Society, were among the pall-bearers, and the mourners included Reynolds and Paoli. Seldom has the death of a man of letters created such a sense of loss either in the public at large or among his friends. Murphy, the editor of Fielding, and biographer of Garrick, says in his well-known essay that Johnson's death " kept the public mind in agitation beyond all previous example." Those great men, then, who attended his funeral represented not merely themselves and his other friends but the intelligence of the whole nation, which saw in the death of Johnson the fall of one of the mighty in the moral and intellectual Israel.

CHAPTER IV

JOHNSON'S CHARACTER AND CHARACTERISTICS

SOMETHING has already been said in the first chapter of this book about the character of Johnson. The argument of that chapter was that the singular position of Johnson as, in a way, the most national of our men of letters, was due not so much to anything he wrote, or even to anything written about him, as to the quality of his own mind and character, to a sort of central sanity that there was about him which Englishmen like to think of as a thing peculiarly English. We may now pass on to look at this character in a little more detail.

Visitors to St. Paul's Cathedral are sometimes astonished as they walk round the space under the dome to come upon a statue which (but for the roll with a Greek inscription upon it) would appear to be that of a retired gladiator meditating upon a wasted life. They are still more astonished when they see under it an inscription indicating that it represents Johnson. The statue is by Bacon, but is not one of his best works. The figure is, as often in eighteenth-century sculpture, clothed only in a loose robe which leaves legs, arms, and one shoulder bare. But the strangeness for us is not one of costume only. If we know anything of Johnson, we know that he was constantly ill all through his life; and whether we know anything of him or not we are apt to think of a literary man as a delicate, weakly, nervous, and probably valetudinarian sort of person. Nothing can be further from that than the muscular statue. And in this matter the statue is perfectly right. And the fact which it reports is far from being unimportant. The body and the mind are inextricably interwoven in all of us, and certainly in Johnson's case the influence of the body was obvious and conspicuous. His melancholy, his constantly repeated conviction of the general unhappiness of human life, was certainly the result of his constitutional infirmities. On the other hand, his courage, and his entire indifference to pain, were partly due to his great bodily strength. Perhaps the vein of rudeness, almost of fierceness, which sometimes showed itself in his conversation, was the natural temper of an invalid and suffering giant. That at any rate is what he was. He was the victim from childhood of a disease which resembled St. Vitus's Dance. He never knew, Boswell says, " the natural joy of a free and vigorous use of his limbs; when he walked it was like the struggling gait of one in fetters." All accounts agree that his strange gesticulations and contortions were painful for his friends to witness and attracted crowds of starers in the streets. But Reynolds says that he could sit still for his portrait to be taken, and that when his mind was engaged by a conversation the convulsions ceased. In any case, it is certain that neither this perpetual misery, nor his constant fear of losing his reason, nor his many grave attacks of illness, ever induced him to surrender the privileges that belonged to his physical strength. He justly thought no character so disagreeable as that of a valetudinarian, and was determined not to be one himself. He had known what it was to live on fourpence halfpenny a day and scorned the life of sofa cushions and beef-tea into which well-attended old gentlemen so easily slip. Once, when Mrs. Thrale asked him how he was, his reply was " Ready to become a scoundrel, Madam " (his word for a self-indulgent invalid); " with a little more spoiling you will make me a complete rascal." But in that she never succeeded. Rather he carried the war into her camp, and when they were driving together would never allow her to complain of rain, dust, or any such inconveniences. " How do other people bear them ? " he would ask, and would treat those who talked of such topics as evidently having nothing intelligent to say. " A mill that goes without grist is as good a companion as such creatures," he once broke out. He required no valeting, or nursing; bathed at Brighton in October when he was nearing sixty, refused to be carried to land by the boatmen at Iona, as Boswell and Sir Allan Maclean were, but sprang into the sea and waded ashore; would not change his clothes when he got wet at Inverary; was a hundred years before his time in his love of open windows, and rode fifty miles with fox-hounds, only to declare that hunting was a dull business and that its popularity merely showed the paucity of human pleasures.

Mrs. Thrale says that no praise ever pleased him more than when some one said of him on Brighton Downs, "Why, Johnson rides as well as the most illiterate fellow in England." He was always eager to show that his legs and arms could do as much as other people's. When he was past sixty-six he ran a race in the rain at Paris with his friend Baretti. He insisted on rolling down a hill like a schoolboy when staying with Langton in Lincolnshire : once at Lichfield when he was over seventy he slipped away from his friends to find a railing he used to jump when he was a boy, threw away his coat, hat, and wig, and, as he reported with pride, leapt over it twice; and on another occasion at Oxford was bold enough to challenge a Fellow, "eminent for learning and worth," and "of an ancient and respectable family in Berkshire," to climb over a wall with him. Apparently, however, the climbing did not actually take place, for the dignified person very properly refused to compromise his dignity.

It is evident that this runner of races and climber of walls was very far from being the sedentary weakling, afraid to enjoy the pleasures of the body or face its pains, in whom popular imagination fancies it sees the man of letters. No man was ever more fearless of

H

pain than Johnson. The only thing he was afraid of was death. Of the extent and even violence of that fear in him till within a few days of the actual event, the evidence, in spite of what Sir Walter Raleigh has said, is conclusive and overwhelming. It comes from every one who knew him. But that was a moral and intellectual fear. Of physical fear he knew nothing. The knife of the surgeon had terrors then which our generation has happily forgotten. But it had none for Johnson. When he lay dying his only fear was that his doctors, one of whom he called " timidorum timidissimus," would spare him pain which if inflicted might have prolonged his life. He called to them to cut deeper when they were operating, and finally took the knife into his own hands and did for himself what he thought the surgeon had failed to do. " I will be conquered, I will not capitulate," were his words : and he acted on them till the very last days were come.

Nor was this courage merely desperation in the presence of the great Terror. He was as brave in health as in illness. He was perfectly quiet and unconcerned during a dangerous storm between Skye and Mull; and on being told that it was doubtful whether they would make for Mull or Col cheerfully replied, " Col for my money." Roads in

those days were not what they are now :
but he never would admit that accidents
could happen and pooh-poohed them when
they did. Nor was his courage merely
passive. Beauclerk did not find it so when
at his country house he saw Johnson go up
to two large dogs which were fighting and
beat them till they stopped : nor did Langton
when he warned Johnson against a dangerous
pool where they were bathing, only to see
Johnson swim straight into it; nor did the
four ruffians who once attacked him in the
street and were surprised to find him more
than a match for the four of them. Whoever
trifled with him was apt to learn sooner than
he wished that *nemo me impune lacessit* was
a saying which was to be taken very literally
from Johnson's mouth. Garrick used to tell
a story of a man who took a chair which had
been placed for Johnson at the Lichfield
theatre and refused to give it up when asked,
upon which Johnson simply tossed man and
chair together into the pit. He proposed to
treat Foote, the comic actor, in much the same
way. Hearing of Foote's intention to carica-
ture him on the stage he suddenly at dinner
asked Davies, a friend of Foote's, "what was
the common price of an oak stick," and being
answered sixpence, "Why then, sir (said he),
give me leave to send your servant to purchase

a shilling one. I'll have a double quantity; for I am told Foote means to take me off, as he calls it, and I am determined the fellow shall not do it with impunity." The threat was sufficient; as Johnson said, "he knew I would have broken his bones." Years afterwards Foote, perhaps in half-conscious revenge, amused himself by holding Johnson up to ridicule in a private company at Edinburgh. Unluckily for him Boswell was present and naturally felt Foote's behaviour an act of rudeness to himself. So he intervened and pleaded that Johnson must be allowed to have some sterling wit, adding that he had heard him say a very good thing about Foote himself. "Ah," replied the unwary Foote, "my old friend Sam; no man says better things : do let us have it." On which Boswell related how he had once said to Johnson when they were talking of Foote, "Pray, sir, is not Foote an infidel ? " to which Johnson had replied, "I do not know, sir, that the fellow is an infidel; but if he be an infidel, he is an infidel as a dog is an infidel; that is to say, he has never thought upon the subject." Boswell's story was as effective as his master's stick. There was no more question that night of taking off Johnson : Foote had enough to do to defend himself against the cannonade of laughter that Boswell had brought upon him.

A man of the mettle Johnson shows in those stories was certain to have no more fears about defending the public than about defending himself. So when he thought the so-called poems of Ossian a fabrication he said so everywhere without hesitation; and when their editor or author Macpherson, finding other methods fail, tried to silence him by bluster and threats, he received the reply which is only less famous than its author's letter to Lord Chesterfield.

"MR. JAMES MACPHERSON,

"I received your foolish and impudent letter. Any violence offered me I shall do my best to repel; and what I cannot do for myself, the law shall do for me. I hope I shall never be deterred from detecting what I think a cheat, by the menaces of a ruffian.

"What would you have me retract? I thought your book an imposture; I think it an imposture still. For this opinion I have given my reasons to the public, which I here dare you to refute. Your rage I defy. Your abilities, since your Homer, are not so formidable, and what I hear of your morals inclines me to pay regard not to what you shall say but to what you shall prove. You may print this if you will.

"SAM. JOHNSON."

The first thing then to get clear about Johnson is that there was a very vigorous animal at the base of the mind and soul that we know in his books and in his talk. Part of the universal interest he has inspired lies in that. The people who put off the body in this life may be divine, though that is far from certain, but they are apt to affect us little because we do not feel them to be human. There is much in Johnson—a turn for eating seven or eight peaches in the garden before breakfast, for instance—which gives unregenerate beings like schoolboys a feeling of confidence at once. And older persons, not yet altogether regenerate, are apt to have a weakness for a man who was willing to be knocked up at three in the morning by some young roysterers, and turn out with them for a "frisk" about the streets and taverns and down the river in a boat. The "follies of the wise" are never altogether follies. Johnson at midnight outside the Temple roaring with Gargantuan laughter that echoed from Temple Bar to what we now call Ludgate Circus is a picture his wisest admirers would be slowest to forget. The laugh and the frisk and the peaches are so many hall-marks to assure us that the philosopher is still a man and has not forgotten that he was once a boy : that he has always had five senses like the rest of us ; and that if he bids us take a grave view of life it is not because he knows nothing about it.

Another note of catholicity in Johnson is his wide experience of social conditions. The man in him never for an instant disappeared in the " gentleman." Very few of our great men of letters have ever known poverty in the real sense of the word, in the way the really poor know it. Johnson had, and he never forgot it. It is true that like most people who have known what it is to be uncertain about to-morrow's dinner he did not much care to talk about these experiences. No one does perhaps except politicians who find them useful bids for popularity at a mass meeting. Johnson at any rate when he had arrived at comparatively easy social conditions frankly admitted that he did not like " low life." His sympathy with the poor, was, as we shall see, one of the strongest things in him, and made one of the deepest marks in his actual life; but he never thought it necessary to indulge in polite or political fictions about the superior virtue or wisdom of the working class. " Poverty," he once wrote in words that come at first sight rather startlingly from the mouth of so strictly Biblical a Christian as he, " is a great enemy to human happiness . . . it makes some virtues impracticable and others extremely difficult."

" Of riches," he said on another occasion, " it is not necessary to write the praise." No doubt the opposition between such remarks as these, meant as Johnson meant them, and certain sayings in the Gospels, is like the opposition between many contrasted pairs of sayings in the New Testament itself, more verbal than real. But it is as strong a proof as could be given of the power and universality in the eighteenth century of the temper which Butler called " cool and reasonable," the temper which hated and despised " enthusiasm," that such a man as Johnson, a man, too, who owed his religious faith to Law's *Serious Call*, could use such words without the slightest consciousness of their needing explanation.

The fact is that Johnson never, even in his religion, left his open eye or his common sense behind him : and common sense told him, what a brighter light concealed from St. Francis but the history of his Order was to show too plainly within half a century of his death, that poverty is at least for ordinary men no assured school of the Christian virtues. Johnson's attitude towards the poor, in fact, included the whole of sympathy and understanding but not one tittle of sentiment. They had the benefit of the greater part of his small income; he gave constantly, both to those who had claims on him and to those who had none, really loving the poor, says Mrs. Thrale, " as I never yet saw any one else do, with an earnest desire to make them happy," and insisting on giving them, not merely relief, but indulgence and pleasure. He wished them to have something more than board and lodging, some "sweeteners of their existence," and he was not always frightened if the sweeteners preferred were gin and tobacco. His very home he made into a retreat, as Mrs. Thrale says with little exaggeration, for "the lame, the blind, the sad and the sorrowful "; and he gave these humble friends more than board and lodging, treating them with at least as ceremonious a civility as he would have used to so many people of fashion.

He held no theories of political or social equality; on the contrary, he looked upon such theories as mischievous nonsense : but the respect paid to him in his later years by great personages never made him take a Mayfair or "county-family" view of life. He might stay at Inverary, visit Alnwick and be invited to Chatsworth, but it took more than the civilities of three Dukes to blind him to the fact that on a map of humanity all the magnates in the world occupy but a small space. Even in the days when he lived at

his ease in a rich man's house and, when in
his own, would dine out every day for a fort-
night, he never surrendered himself, as so
many who have at last reached comfort do,
to the subtle unrealities of the drawing-room.
He would not allow the well-do-to to call
themselves " the world " : and when Sir
Joshua said one day that nobody wore laced
coats any longer and that once everybody
had worn them, " See now," said Johnson,
" how absurd that is; as if the bulk of mankind consisted of fine gentlemen that came to
him to sit for their pictures. If every man
who wears a laced coat (that he can pay for)
was extirpated, who would miss them ? "
So when Mrs. Thrale once complained of the
smell of cooking he told her she was a fortunate
woman never to have experienced the delight
of smelling her dinner beforehand. " Which
pleasure," she answered, " is to be enjoyed
in perfection by such as have the happiness
to pass through Porridge Island of a morning ! " Johnson's answer was the grave
rebuke of a man from whose mind the darker
side of a prosperous world was never long
absent. " Come, come, let's have no sneering
at what is serious to so many : hundreds of
your fellow-creatures, dear lady, turn another
way that they may not be tempted by the
luxuries of Porridge Island to wish for gratifi-

cations they are not able to obtain : you are
certainly not better than all of them : give
God thanks that you are happier." It is
Mrs. Thrale who herself tells the story : and
it is to her credit that she calls Johnson's
answer a just rebuke.

But Johnson's equality was that of the
moralist, not that of the politician. He was
the exact opposite of a leveller, believing in
the distinction of ranks as not only a necessity
of society, but an addition to its strength and
to the variety and interest of its life. He
himself scrupulously observed the formalities
of social respect, and would no doubt, like
Mr. Gladstone, have repudiated with horror
the idea of being placed at dinner above the
obscurest of peers. His bow to an Archbishop
is described as a studied elaboration of
temporal and spiritual homage, and he once
went so far as to imply that nothing would
induce him to contradict a Bishop. There
no doubt he promised more than the presence
of a stupid Bishop or a Whig Bishop would
have allowed him to perform. For no considerations of rank ever prevented him from
expressing his own opinions or trampling upon
those of other people. Except Swift, perhaps,
he was the most independent man that ever
lived. Of Swift's jealous and angry arrogance
he had nothing. But he was full of what he

himself called " defensive pride." That was his answer when he was accused of showing at least as much pride as Lord Chesterfield in the affair of the Dictionary; " but mine," he said, " was defensive pride." He was always on his guard against the very appearance of accepting the patronage of the great. Even Thackeray's Argus eye could not have detected a grain of snobbery in him. At Inverary he would not let Boswell call before dinner lest it should look like fishing for an invitation; and when he dined there the next day and sat next the Duke, he did not refrain, even in that Whig holy of holies, from chaffing about one of the Campbells who " had been bred a violent Whig but afterwards kept better company and became a Tory " ! So once, when he dined at Bowood with Lord Shelburne he refused to repeat a story at the request of his host, saying that he would not be dragged in as story-teller to the company. And he would never give the authority for any fact he mentioned, if the authority happened to be a lord. Indeed he carried his sturdy independence so far that in his last years he fancied that his company was no longer desired in these august circles. " I never courted the great," he said; " they sent for me, but I think they now give me up "; adding, in reply to Boswell's polite disbelief, " No, sir; great lords and great ladies don't love to have their mouths stopped."

Here again Johnson represented the typical Englishman as foreigners then and since have read his character. An accepter and respecter of rank as a social fact and a political principle, he was as proud in his way as the proudest man in the land. Tory as he was, for him every freeborn Englishman was one of the " lords of human kind " : a citizen of no mean city, but of one in which—

" . . . e'en the peasant boasts these rights
    to scan,
And learns to venerate himself as man ! "

He had all an Englishman's pride in England, as was prettily seen in his reply to Mrs. Thrale in the theatre at Versailles; " Now we are here what shall we act, Dr. Johnson ? The Englishman at Paris ? " " No, no; we will try to act Harry the Fifth "; and at bottom he thought that a free Englishman was too great a man to be patronized by any one on earth.

But there was something better than pride at the root of his whole attitude towards the rich and the poor ; and that was his humanity. Again and again, as one studies him, one comes back to that, his humanity, his love of men as men. It was that which made him one of the earliest and fiercest enemies of the slave trade. So early as 1740 he maintained the natural right of the negroes to liberty; and he once startled "some very grave men at Oxford" by giving as his toast "Here's to the next insurrection of the negroes in the West Indies." This was his invariable attitude from first to last, and it was no mere scoring of a party point against the Americans when he asked, in *Taxation No Tyranny*, "How is it that we hear the loudest yelps for liberty among the drivers of negroes?" No Tory prejudices and no sophistical arguments were ever able to silence in him the voice of common humanity. He spared his own country no more than the American rebels, describing Jamaica as "a den of tyrants and a dungeon of slaves," and speaking indignantly of the thousands of black men "who are now repining under English cruelty." He denounced, as not only wicked but also absurd and foolish, the opinion common among the "English barbarians that cultivate the southern islands of America," that savages are to be regarded as scarcely distinct from animals; and he dreaded discoveries of new lands because he was always afraid they would result in conquest and cruelty.

And this was not the public and vicarious

humanity with which we are too familiar. What he preached to others he practised himself. He loved all life and all the men and women whom he saw living it. It takes one's breath away at first to find the grave moralist of *The Rambler* coolly saying to Mrs. Thrale and Fanny Burney, " Oh, I loved Bet Flint ! " just after he had frankly explained to them that that lady was " habitually a slut and a drunkard and occasionally a thief and a harlot." But the creature was what we call a " character," had had many curious adventures, and had written her life in verse and brought it to Johnson to correct, an offer which he had declined, giving her half a crown instead which she " liked as well." He had, in fact, got below the perhaps superficial slut and harlot to the aboriginal human being, and that once arrived at he never forgot it. Nor did he need the kindly humours of old acquaintance to enable him to discover it. No moral priggishness dried up the tenderness with which he regarded the most forlorn specimens of humanity. Boswell tells this story. " Coming home late one night he found a poor woman lying in the street, so much exhausted that she could not walk : he took her upon his back and carried her to his house, where he discovered that she was one of those wretched females who had fallen into the lowest state of vice, poverty and disease. Instead of harshly upbraiding her he had her taken care of with all tenderness for a long time at considerable expense till she was restored to health, and endeavoured to put her into a virtuous way of living." Like Mr. Gladstone, he exposed his own character to suspicion by his kindness to such poor creatures as this. His heart was always open to the miserable, so that Goldsmith said that the fact of being miserable was enough to " ensure the protection of Johnson." Sir John Hawkins says that, when some one asked him how he could bear to have his house full of " necessitous and undeserving people," his reply was, " If I did not assist them no one else would, and they must be lost for want." He always declared that the true test of a nation's civilization was the state of its poor, and specially directed Boswell to report to him how the poor were maintained in Holland. When his mother's old servant lay dying he went to say good-bye to her and prayed with her, while she, as he says, " held up her poor hands as she lay in bed with great fervour." Then, after the prayer, " I kissed her. She told me that to part was the greatest pain that she had ever felt and that she hoped we should meet again in a better place. I expressed, with swelled eyes and great emotion of tenderness, the same hope. We kissed and parted. I humbly hope to meet again and to part no more."

Let all pictures of Johnson as a harsh and arrogant bully fade away before this touching little scene. The truth is that at the root of the man there was an unfailing spring of human love. One who knew him very well said that peace and goodwill were the natural emanations of his heart. All sorts of weakness found a friend in him. He was markedly kind to children, especially little girls, to servants, to animals. When he was himself in great poverty he would put pennies in the hands of the children sleeping on doorsteps in the Strand, as he walked home in the small hours of the morning. He left most of his property to his negro servant Frank : and so united a delicate consideration for Frank's feelings with an affection for his cat Hodge that he always went out himself to buy oysters for Hodge lest Frank should think himself insulted by being employed to wait upon a cat.

Nor did this human and social element in him show itself only in such grave shape as hatred of slavery and tenderness to the poor. His sense of kinship with other men was, indeed, a serious conviction held on serious grounds. But it was also the expression of his natural good nature, and overflowed into

I

the obvious channels of kindly sociability which come to every man unsought, as well as into these deeper ones of sympathy which are only found by those who seek them. Those who know him only through Boswell are in danger of over-accentuating the graver side of his character. In Boswell's eyes he was primarily the sage and saint, and though he exhibits him playing many other parts as well it is on these two that the stress is especially laid. Other people, notably Fanny Burney, who in his last years saw a great deal of him at the Thrales', enable us to restore the balance. She loved and honoured him with an affection and reverence only short of Boswell's : and her youth, cleverness and charm won Johnson's heart as no one won it who came so late into his world. Like Boswell she had a touch of literary genius, and luckily for us she used it partly to write about Johnson. Hers is the most vivid picture we have of him after Boswell's, and it is notable that she is for ever laying stress on his gaiety. The seriousness is there, and she thoroughly appreciated it; but the thing that strikes any one coming to her from Boswell is the perpetual recurrence of such phrases as " Dr. Johnson was gaily sociable," " Dr. Johnson was in high spirits, full of mirth and sport," " Dr. Johnson was in exceeding humour."

On one day in 1778 he appears in her journal as " so facetious that he challenged Mr. Thrale to get drunk "; and the next year, when he was seventy, she writes that he " has more fun and comical humour and love of nonsense about him than almost anybody I ever saw." Even in 1783, after he had had the stroke which was the beginning of the end, she speaks of his " gaiety." The explanation is no doubt partly that Miss Burney was a woman and saw him chiefly with women, Boswell a man who saw him chiefly with men. Even without her genius she would not be the first young woman whose admiring affection has seemed to an old man to give him back his youth. And she had not only her own sudden and surprising celebrity but all that happy ease of the Streatham life, and the cleverness and good humour of Mrs. Thrale, to help her. No wonder Johnson was at his brightest in such circumstances.

But his easy sociability there was no sudden revolution in his nature. Sir John Hawkins, who, though never a very congenial companion, had known him longer than almost any of his friends, says of him that he was " a great contributor to the mirth of conversation." And constant glimpses of his lighter side are caught all through Boswell, such as that picture of him at Corrichatachin, in Skye,

I 2

sitting with a young Highland lady on his knee and kissing her. We have already heard his peals of midnight laughter ringing through the silent Strand. The truth is that both by nature and by principle he was a very sociable man. That is another of the elements in his permanent popularity. The man who liked all sorts and conditions of men when he was alive has one of the surest passports to the friendliness of posterity. Johnson, like Walter Scott, could and did talk to everybody, or, rather, join in any talk that anybody started; for he seldom spoke first even among his friends. It was probably to this ease of intercourse that he owed the stores of information with which he often surprised his hearers on all sorts of unlikely subjects, such as on one occasion that of the various purposes to which bones picked up in the streets by the London poor are put, and the use of a particular paste in melting iron. But in these casual conversations he was not consciously seeking information as Scott partly was; he was just giving play to his natural sociability, or perhaps deliberately acting on the principle of *humani nihil*, which no one ever held more strongly than he.

He always condemned the cold reserve so common among Englishmen. Two strangers of any other nation, he used to say, will find

some topic of talk at once when they are
thrown into an inn parlour together : two
Englishmen will go each to a different window
and remain in obstinate silence. " Sir, we as
yet do not enough understand the common
rights of humanity." He boasted that he
was never strange in a strange place, and
would talk at his best in a coach with perfect
strangers to their outspoken amazement and
delight. At all times he hated and dreaded
being alone, both on moral and medical
grounds, having the fear of madness always
before him. He said that he had only once
refused to dine out for the sake of his studies,
and then he had done nothing. He praised
a tavern chair as the throne of human felicity,
better indeed, because freer, than anything
to be found at a private house; for only " a
very impudent dog indeed can freely command
what is in another man's house." He loved
to assert that all great kings (among whom he
curiously included Charles II, " the last King
of England who was a man of parts ") had been
social men; and he was the most convinced
of Londoners because it was in London that
life, which to him meant the exercise of the
social and intellectual faculties, was to be
found at its eagerest and fullest. If, as Mrs.
Thrale said, all he asked for happiness was
conversation it must be admitted that his

standard was exacting both in quantity and quality. He never wanted to go to bed, and if any one would stay with him, would sit talking and drinking tea till four in the morning. Yet his instantaneous severity in reproving inaccuracies or refuting fallacies was so alarming that he sometimes reduced a whole company to the silence of fear. The last thing he wished, no doubt, but it is one of the tragedies of life that power will not be denied its exercise, even to its own misery. But these were the rare dark moments; as a rule, as we have seen, all who came into a room with him were entranced by the force, variety and brilliance of his talk.

His natural turn was to be the very opposite of a killjoy; he loved not merely to be kind to others but to be " merry " with them, Mrs. Thrale tells us : loved to join in children's games, especially those of a " knot of little misses," of whom he was fonder than of boys : and always encouraged cards, dancing and similar amusements. He was by temperament and conviction a conformer to the innocent ways of the world : and once, when some Quaker was denouncing the vanities of dress, he broke out, " Oh, let us not be found when our Master calls us, ripping the lace off our waistcoats, but the spirit of contention from our souls and tongues ! . . . Alas, sir, a man who cannot get to heaven in a green coat will not find his way thither the sooner in a grey one." Though he practised some severities, such as fasting, himself, he was altogether opposed to an austere view of life : was no friend, he said, to making religion appear too hard, by which he thought many good people had done harm. Though he walked with enthusiastic reverence on any ground trodden by saints or hermits, yet he was quite clear that retirement from the world was for ordinary men and women both a mistake and a crime; and he regarded with special distrust all " youthful passion for abstracted devotion." The Carthusian silence was, of course, particularly obnoxious to the master and lover of talk. " We read in the Gospel," he said, " of the apostles being sent to preach, but not to hold their tongues." We all like to find reasons of religion or philosophy in justification of our own pleasures : and no doubt one hears the personal prejudices of the lover of society as well as the serious thought of the student of life in the warmth with which he denounces solitude as " dangerous to reason without being favourable to virtue," and declares that " the solitary mortal is certainly luxurious, probably superstitious, and possibly mad."

But real as the social element in Johnson

was, and important as the remembrance of
it is for a corrective of the too solemn portrait
of him for which Boswell gives some excuse,
it never got the mastery of him. In the
ordinary way the life of the pre-eminently
social man or woman gradually disappears
in a dancing sunshine of sociability. The
butterfly finds crossing and recrossing other
butterflies in the airy, flowery spaces of the
world such a pleasant business that it asks
no more : above all, it does not care to ask
the meaning of a thing so easy and agreeable
as day to day existence. The pleasures and
the business that lie on life's surface, the
acquaintances and half friends that are
encountered there, are enough for it : and
the crowded empty days glide by as easily
and as imperceptibly as a boatful of dreaming
idlers drifting on unawares till the pace
suddenly quickens for a moment, and almost
before the speed wakens them they are
struggling hopelessly in the whirlpool at the
bottom of the fall. But, for Johnson, society
had no sleeping potion strong enough to over-
come his ever-wakeful sense of the issues of
life. Underneath all the " gaiety " that Miss
Burney liked to record, there was one of the
gravest of men, a man whose religion had a
strong " Day of Judgment " element in it,
who believed as literally as Bunyan in heaven

and hell as the alternative issues of life, except that he allowed himself some Catholic latitude of hope as to that third possibility which provides the most human of the three divisions of Dante's great poem. Most people, even the most strictly orthodox, would now say that Johnson's religion contained too much consciousness of the Divine Judgment and too little of the Divine Love. But at least the fear of God, which was to him a thing so real and awful, had nothing in it of the attitude, so common in all ages and all religions of the world, which attempts to delude or defeat or buy off the hostility of a capricious despot by means of money, or magical arts, or a well devised system of celestial alliances. In Johnson it came simply from the sense of sin and issued in the desire to live better. He was as ethically minded as any one in that moralizing century : only that he added to ethics the faith in God and conviction of sin which have a power on life unknown to mere moral philosophy. He lived among good men, mainly, but men, for the most part, whose intellectual attitude towards the Christian faith was one of detachment, indifference, or conventional acquiescence. That could not be his attitude. He was the last man in the world to be content with anything nebulous. The active exercise of thinking was to him a pleasure in all matters, and in things important a duty as well. He was certain not to avoid it in the most important question of all. He might have been either Hume or Butler, either Wesley or Gibbon, but he was certain not to be, what the average cultivated man in his day was, a respectable but unenthusiastic and unconvinced conformer. Conventional acquiescence is easy provided a man does not choose to think or inquire; but, as Carlyle said, that would not do for Johnson: he always zealously recommended and practised inquiry. The result was what is well known. His mind settled definitely on the opposite side to Hume and Gibbon : the Christian religion became intensely real to him, sometimes, it almost seems, the nightmare of his life, often its comfort and strength, present, at any rate, audibly and visibly, in every company where he was; for no man was ever so little ashamed of his religion as Johnson. It was the principle of his life in public as well as in private. Hence that spectacle which Carlyle found so memorable, of " Samuel Johnson, in the era of Voltaire able to purify and fortify his soul, and hold real Communion with the Highest, in the Church of St. Clement Danes; a thing to be looked at with pity, admiration, awe."

That church still remains; the least altered,

perhaps, with the possible exception of the house in Gough Square, of all the buildings which once had the body of Johnson inside them; a place of pilgrimage for many Johnsonians who, refusing to be driven away by the commonplace window which officially honours his memory, are grateful to find the seat he used to occupy marked out for their veneration : and not altogether ungrateful even for the amateur statue which stands in the churchyard, looking towards his beloved Fleet Street. There were performed the central acts of those half tragic Good Fridays, those self-condemning Easter Days, recorded in his private note-books : there, on the Good Friday of 1773, he took Boswell with him, and Boswell observed, what he said he should never forget, " the tremulous earnestness with which Johnson pronounced the awful petition in the Litany : ' In the hour of death, and at the day of judgment, good Lord deliver us.' "

We now know more in some ways about his religious life than his friends did, because we have the private prayers he wrote for his own use, the sermons he composed for others, and a few notes, chiefly of a religious kind, describing his doings and feelings on certain days of his life. But all the evidence, private and public, points the same way. His prayers are among the best in English, pulsing and throbbing with earnest faith and fear, yet entirely free from the luscious sentimentality of so many modern religious compositions. He was in the habit of making special prayers for all important occasions : he made them, for instance, sometimes before he entered upon new literary undertakings, as in the case of *The Rambler;* and he took Boswell into the Church at Harwich and prayed with him before he saw him off for Utrecht. No one who was with him on such occasions failed to be impressed by his profound and awe-inspiring sincerity. Mrs. Thrale says that when he repeated the *Dies Irae* " he never could pass the stanza ending *Tantus labor non sit cassus* without bursting into a flood of tears "; and another witness records how one night at a dinner where some one quoted the nineteenth psalm his worn and harsh features were transformed, and " his face was almost as if it had been the face of an angel " as he recited Addison's noble version of that psalm. Phrases that came unbidden to his voice or pen show the same constant sense of this life as a thing to be lived in the sight and presence of Eternity. When at Boswell's request he sends him a letter of advice, one of his sentences is " I am now writing, and you, when you read this, are reading, under the Eye of Omnipresence."

So on one occasion he said, " The better a
man is, the more afraid he is of death, having
a clearer view of infinite purity "; and he
would quote Law's remark that " every man
knows something worse of himself than he
is sure of in others." Such sayings do not
come to the lips of men to whom the life of the
spirit and the conscience is not a daily and
hourly reality. That it was to Johnson; and
no one understands him who does not lay
stress on it. It does not always appear in
such grave guise as in these instances, but it
is always there. We may take our leave of
it as we see it in simpler and happier shape in
Boswell's account of himself and Johnson
sharing a bedroom at Glen Morrison. " After
we had offered up our private devotions and
had chatted a little from our beds, Dr. Johnson
said ' God bless us both for Jesus Christ's
sake ! Good-night.' I pronounced ' Amen.'
He fell asleep immediately."

A serious conviction held by a human being
is generally found to be an inner citadel
surrounded by a network of prejudices. It
was only Johnson's intimate friends who were
admitted into the central fortress of his faith:
the rest of the world saw it plainly indeed,
but did not get nearer than the girdle of defensive prejudices outside, and to them they

often got nearer than they liked. Whether
people discovered that Johnson was a Christian or not, they were quite certain to discover
that he was a Churchman. His High Church
and Tory guns were always ready for action,
and Lord Auchinleck is perhaps the only
recorded assailant who succeeded in silencing
them. The praise he gave to the dearest of
his friends, " He hated a fool, he hated a
rogue, and he hated a Whig : he was a very
good hater," was exactly applicable to himself.
For us the word Whig has come to mean a
dignified aristocrat who, by the pressure of
family tradition, maintains a painful association with vulgar Radicals : for Johnson it
meant a rebel against the principle of authority. From that point of view he was
accustomed to say with perfect justice that
the first Whig was the Devil. His sallies at
the general expense of the enemies of " Church
and King " must not be confused with those
on many other subjects, as, for instance, on
the Scotch, which were partly humorous in
intention as well as in expression. He
trounced the Scotch to annoy Boswell and
amuse himself. He trounced Whigs, Quakers
and Presbyterians because he loved authority
both in Church and State. These latter outbursts represented definite opinions which
were held, as usually happens, with all the

more passion because reason had not been allowed to play her full part in their maturing. Johnson could hold no views to which he had not been able to supply a rational foundation : but in these matters passion had been given a free hand in the superstructure.

In this way his Tory outbursts have a smack of life about them not always to be found in the utterances of sages. High Tories were not often seen in the intellectual London world of these days : they were to be found rather in country parsonages and college common-rooms. In London Whiggery sat enthroned and complacent. It is, therefore, with a pleasant sense of the fluttering of Whig dovecotes that we watch Johnson, always, as Miss Burney said, the first man in any company in which he appeared, startling superior persons by taking the high Tory tone. He once astonished an old gentleman to whose niece he was talking by saying to her, " My dear, I hope you are a Jacobite "; and answered the uncle's protest by saying, " Why, sir, I meant no offence to your niece, I meant her a great compliment. A Jacobite, sir, believes in the divine right of kings. He that believes in the divine right of kings believes in a Divinity. A Jacobite believes in the divine right of Bishops. He that believes in the divine right of Bishops believes in the divine authority of the Christian religion. Therefore, sir, a Jacobite is neither an Atheist nor a Deist. That cannot be said of a Whig: for *Whiggism is a negation of all principle.*" But it was not often that his Toryism expressed itself in anything so like a chain of reasoning as this. As a rule, it appears rather in those conversational sallies, so pleasantly compounded of wrath, humour, and contempt, which are the most remembered thing about him. It provides some of the most characteristic; as the dry answer to Boswell who expressed his surprise at having met a Staffordshire Whig, a being whom he had not supposed to exist, " Sir, there are rascals in all countries "; or the answer Garrick got when he asked him " Why did not you make me a Tory, when we lived so much together ? " " Why," said Johnson, pulling a heap of halfpence from his pocket, " did not the King make these guineas ? " Or the true story he liked to tell of Boswell who, he said, " in the year 1745 was a fine boy, wore a white cockade, and prayed for King James, till one of his uncles gave him a shilling on condition that he should pray for King George, which he accordingly did. So you see that *Whigs of all ages are made the same way.*" In the same vein is his pleasant good-bye to Burke at Beaconsfield before the election of 1774,

" Farewell, my dear sir, I wish you all the success which can possibly be wished you—*by an honest man.*" Even the fiercer outburst about Patriotism (that is according to the meaning of the word in those days, the pretence of preferring the interests of the people to those of the Crown), " Patriotism is the last refuge of a scoundrel," takes for us an added piquancy from the fact that Charles Fox, already a " patriot," and soon to be the greatest of all, was in the Chair at " The Club " on the night when it was uttered.

But as a rule the fiercest assaults were reserved for Presbyterians and Dissenters in whom political and ecclesiastical iniquity were united. When he was walking in the ruins of St. Andrews and some one asked where John Knox was buried, he broke out " I hope in the highway. I have been looking at his reformations." And he wished a dangerous steeple not to be taken down, " for," said he, " it may fall on some of the posterity of John Knox : and no great matter ! " So when he and Boswell went to the Episcopal church at Montrose he gave " a shilling extraordinary " to the Clerk, saying, " He belongs to an honest church," and when Boswell rashly reminded him that Episcopalians were only dissenters, that is, only *tolerated*, in Scotland, he brought down upon

K

himself the crushing retort, " Sir, we are here as Christians in Turkey." These ingeniously exact analogies were always a favourite weapon with him; and perhaps the most brilliant of them all is one he used on this same subject in reply to Robertson, who said to him in London, " Dr. Johnson, allow me to say that in one respect I have the advantage of you; when you were in Scotland you would not come to hear any of our preachers, whereas, when I am here, I attend your public worship without scruple, and, indeed, with great satisfaction." " Why, sir," said Johnson, " that is not so extraordinary : the King of Siam sent ambassadors to Louis the Fourteenth : but Louis the Fourteenth sent none to the King of Siam." This topic also enjoys another distinction. It is one of many proofs of the superlative excellence of Johnson's talk that it cannot be imitated. Hundreds of clever men have made the attempt, but, with the exception of a single sentence, not one of these manufactured utterances could impose for an instant upon a real Johnsonian. That single exception deals with this same anti-Presbyterian prejudice. It is variously asscribed to Thorold Rogers and to Birkbeck Hill, the most Johnsonian of all men. It supposes that Boswell and Johnson are walking in Oxford, and Boswell, endowed with the gift of prophecy, asks Johnson what he would say if he were told that a hundred years after his death the Oxford University Press would allow his Dictionary to be re-edited by a Scotch Presbyterian. " Sir," replies Johnson, " to be facetious it is not necessary to be indecent." Here and here alone is something which might deceive the very elect.

In several of these last utterances the bias is as much anti-Scotch as anti-Presbyterian. Of course Johnson, as his *Journey to the Western Islands* amply proves, had no serious feeling against Scotchmen as Scotchmen like the settled convictions which made him dislike Presbyterians. But then, as always, the Scot had a specially " gude conceit " of himself and a clannish habit of pushing the interest of his brother Scots wherever he went, so that it was commonly thought that to let a Scot into your house or business was not only to let in one conceited fellow, but to be certain of half a dozen more to follow. The English were then still so far from their present admiring acceptance of Scotsmen as their ordinary rulers in Church and State that they had not even begun to think of them as their equals. Scotland was at that time a very poor country, and the poor relation has

K 2

never been a popular character anywhere.
Consequently Englishmen—and who was ever
more English than Johnson ?—commonly saw
in the newly arrived Scot a pauper and an
upstart come to live upon his betters : and
they revenged themselves in the manner
natural to rich relations.   To Johnson's
tongue, too, the Scots offered the important
additional temptations of being often Whigs,
oftener still Presbyterians, and always the
countrymen of Boswell.   This last was probably the one which he found it most impossible
to resist.   Happily Boswell had the almost
unique good sense to enjoy a good thing even
at the expense of his country or himself.   It
is to him, or perhaps at him, that the majority
of these Scotch witticisms were uttered : it
is by him that nearly all of them are recorded,
from the original sally which was the first
sentence he heard from Johnson's lips, in
reply to his " Mr. Johnson, I do indeed come
from Scotland, but I cannot help it."   " That,
sir, I find, is what a very great many of your
countrymen cannot help "—to the famous
reply at the Wilkes dinner, when some one
said " Poor old England is lost,"—" Sir, it
is not so much to be lamented that old
England is lost as that the Scotch have found
it."

On this topic Johnson would always let

himself go. Again and again the generous connoisseurship of Boswell describes not only the witticism but the joyous gusto with which it was uttered. On no subject is the great talker's amazing ingeniousness of retort more conspicuous. When Boswell most justly criticized the absurd extravagance of his famous sentence about the death of Garrick eclipsing the gaiety of nations, Johnson replied, " I could not have said more nor less. It is the truth; *eclipsed,* not *extinguished ;* and his death *did* eclipse; it was like a storm." *Boswell.* " But why nations ? Did his gaiety extend further than his own nation ? " *Johnson.* " Why, sir, some exaggeration must be allowed. Besides nations may be said— if we allow the Scotch to be a nation, and to have gaiety—which they have not." So when Johnson said the Scotch had none of the luxuries or conveniences of life before the Union, and added, " laughing," says Boswell, " with as much glee as if Monboddo had been present," " We have taught you and we'll do the same in time to all barbarous nations— to the Cherokees—and at last to the Ourang-outangs," Boswell tried to meet him by saying " We had wine before the Union." But this only got him into worse trouble. " No, sir, you had some weak stuff, the refuse of France, which would not make you drunk."

Boswell. " I assure you, sir, there was a great deal of drunkenness." *Johnson.* " No, sir ; there were people who died of dropsies which they contracted in trying to get drunk." This was said as they sailed along the shores of Skye ; and of course the whole tour in Scotland afforded many opportunities for such jests. There was the wall at Edinburgh which by tradition was to fall upon some very learned man, but had been taken down some time before Johnson's visit : " They have been afraid it never would fall," said he. There was St. Giles's at Edinburgh, which provoked the chaffing aside to Robertson, " Come, let me see what was once a church." There were the beauties of Glasgow of which Adam Smith boasted, and provoked the famous question " Pray, sir, have you ever seen Brentford ? " There was the supposed treelessness of Scotland, on which he dwells in the *Journey,* and which once led him to question whether there was a tree between Edinburgh and the English border older than himself ; and to reply to Boswell's suggestion that he ought to be whipped at every tree over 100 years old in that space, " I believe I might submit to it for a baubee ! " It led also to the pleasantry in which he emphasized his conviction that the oak stick he had brought from London was stolen and not

merely lost when it disappeared in Mull;
" Consider, sir, the value of such a *piece of
timber* here."

To-day we think of Scotland as one of the
most beautiful countries in the world and go
there in thousands for that reason.   But that
was not why Johnson went. He had little
pleasure in any landscape scenery, and none
in that of moors and mountains. Indeed
nobody had in those days except Gray.   And
Gray was the last man in whose company
Johnson was likely to be found differing from
his contemporaries. So that though he saw
much of what is finest in the noble scenery
of Scotland, it hardly drew from him a single
word of wonder or delight : and his only
remembered allusion to it is the well-known
sally hurled ten years earlier at the Scotsman
in London who thought to get on safe ground
for the defence of his country by speaking
of her " noble wild prospects," but only drew
upon himself the answer, " I believe, sir, you
have a great many. Norway, too, has noble
wild prospects ; and Lapland is remarkable for
prodigious noble wild prospects. But, sir, let
me tell you, the noblest prospect which a
Scotchman ever sees is the high road that
leads him to London ! "

So dangerous it always was to put a phrase
into Johnson's mouth ! So dangerous above

all to try to make him prefer anything to his beloved London. Perhaps no nation in the world has cared so little about its capital city as the English. When one thinks of the passionate affection lavished on Athens, Rome, Paris, even, strange as it seems to us, on Madrid, one is tempted to accuse the English of dull disloyalty to their own noble capital city. London played, at any rate till the French Revolution, a far more important part in English life than any other capital in the life of any other country. In the reign of Charles II, according to Macaulay, it was seventeen times as large as Bristol, then the second city in the Kingdom; a relative position unique in Europe. And all through our history it had led the nation in politics as well as in commerce. Yet of the best of all tributes to greatness, the praise of great men, it had received singularly little. There is Milton's noble burst of eloquence in the *Areopagitica,* but that is the praise not so much of London as of the religion and politics of London at a particular moment. Spenser's beautiful allusion in the *Prothalamion* to " mery London my most kyndly nurse " and to the " sweet Thames " whom he invites to " run softly till I end my song " is among the few tributes of personal affection paid by our poets to the great city. And it is still true to-day that the tutelary genius of London is none of the great poets : it is Samuel Johnson. At this moment, as these pages are being written, the railway stations of London are filled with picture advertisements of the attractions of the great city. And who is the central figure in the picture that deals with central London ! Not Shakespeare or Milton, but Johnson. The worn, rather sad face, more familiar to Englishmen than that of any other man of letters, with the wig and brown coat to make recognition certain, is chosen as the most useful for their purpose by advertisers probably innocent of any literature, but astute enough in knowing what will attract the people.

Johnson's love of London, however, was of his own sort, quite unlike that of Charles Lamb for instance, or that of such a man as Sir Walter Besant. He cared nothing for architecture, and little for history. Still less had his feeling anything to do with the commercial greatness of London. He had a scholar's contempt for traders as people without ideas fit for rational conversation. The man who scoffed at the " boobies of Birmingham " as unworthy of notice in comparison with the gownsmen of Oxford or even the cathedral citizens of Lichfield, whose experience of commercial men made him declare that " trade could not be managed by those who manage it if it had much difficulty," was not likely to have his imagination fired by talk about London as the centre of the world's commerce. What he cared about was a very different thing. He thought of London as the place in all the world where the pulse of human life beat strongest. There a man could store his mind better than anywhere else : there he could not only live but grow : there more than anywhere else he might escape the self-complacency which leads to intellectual and moral torpor, because there he would be certain to meet not only with his equals but with his superiors. These were grave grounds which he could use in an argument : but a man needs no arguments in justification of the things he likes, and Johnson liked London because it was the home of the intellectual pleasures which to him were the only real pleasures, and which made London for him a heaven upon earth. " He who is tired of London is tired of life," he said on one occasion; and on another, when some one remarked that many people were content to live in the country, he replied, " Sir, it is in the intellectual as in the physical world; we are told by natural philosophers that a body is at rest in the place that is fit for it : they who are content to live in the country are fit for the country." He was not one of them :

he wanted Charing Cross and its " full tide of
human existence," and thought that any one
who had once experienced " the full flow of
London talk " must, if he retired to the
country, " either be contented to turn baby
again and play with the rattle, or he will pine
away like a great fish in a little pond, and die
for want of his usual food."   He was more than
once offered good country livings if he would
take orders, but he knew that he would find
the " insipidity and uniformity " of country
life intolerable : and he stayed on to become
the greatest of Londoners.   There is probably
to this day no book, not a professed piece of
topography, which mentions the names of so
many London streets, squares and churches,
as Boswell's *Life of Johnson.*   Many sights
that Johnson saw we can still see exactly as
he saw them; many, of course, have disappeared; and many are so utterly changed
as to be unrecognizable.   The young poet
may still stand where he and Goldsmith stood
in Poets' Corner and say in his heart with
Johnson—

  "Forsitan et nostrum nomen miscebitur
    istis."

But when he goes on as they did to
Temple Bar, he will find that ancient monument retired into the country and certainly

nothing whatever to remind him of the Jacobite heads still mouldering on it, which gave occasion to Goldsmith's witty turning of his Tory friend's quotation—

> "Forsitan et nostrum nomen miscebitur ISTIS."

But on that holy ground the Johnsonian will hardly miss even Temple Bar. For most of Johnson's haunts and homes, the Mitre and the Cock, the Churches of St. Clement and of the Temple, his houses in Johnson's Court and Gough Square, are or were all hard by : and the memory will be far too busy to allow room for the disappointments and lamentations of the eye

But of course the great characteristic of Johnson is neither love of London nor hatred of Presbyterians, nor any of the other things we have been talking about : it is the love and power of talk. We cannot estimate talk nearly as accurately as we estimate writing : so much that belongs to the word spoken is totally lost when it becomes a word recorded : the light in the eye, the brow raised in scorn or anger, the moving lips whose amusement or contempt is a picture before it is a sound, the infinitely varying weight and tone of the human voice : all that is gone or seen only very darkly through the glass of description. But since the talk itself as written down and the manner of it as described are all we have to judge by : and since as long as we are alive and awake we cannot avoid judging the things and people that interest us, we inevitably form opinions about talkers as well as about writers : and the best opinion of those who know English is undoubtedly that Johnson is the greatest of all recorded talkers. The best of all is very possibly some obscure genius who *caret vate sacro :* but Johnson with the invaluable help of Boswell has beaten him and all the others. What is the essence of his superiority ? Not wisdom or profundity certainly. There, of course, he would be immeasurably surpassed by many men of all nations, notably by Socrates, who is probably the most famous and certainly by far the most influential of talkers. Of course his talk comes to us chiefly through the medium of a man of transcendent genius; and Plato may have transcended his master as well as other things. But on the whole all the evidence goes to show that the talk of Socrates was the force which set ideas in motion, which modified the whole subsequent moral and intellectual life of Greece and Rome, and through them of the world; in fact, that the spoken word of Socrates has played a greater part in the world than any written word whatsoever, except the Gospels and the Korán, both themselves, it may be noted, the record of a spoken word greater than the written book. Beside anything of this kind Johnson sinks of course into entire insignificance. But as an artist in talk, that is a man who talked well for the pleasure of it, as an end in itself, and whose talk was heard gladly as a thing of triumph and delight, bringing with it its own justification, he probably far surpassed Socrates. If he, too, had got to his trial he probably would have been as scornful as Socrates of the judgment of popular opinion. But he never would have got there, not only because he was too conservative to deny the established divinities, but because he was so entertaining that everybody liked listening to him, whatever he denied or affirmed. Socrates, on the other hand, was evidently something of a bore, with a bore's unrelieved earnestness and inopportune persistence. His saying about " letting the talk lead us where it will," is an exact description of Johnson's practice, but nothing could be less like his own. He is always relentlessly guiding it towards a particular goal, from the path to which he will not have it for a moment diverted. Johnson, on the other hand, takes no thought whatever for the argumentative morrow, never starts a subject, never sets out to prove anything. He talks as an artist paints, just for the joy of doing what he is conscious of doing well. The talk, like the picture, is its own sufficient reward.

The same sort of inferiority puts other famous talkers, Coleridge for instance, and Luther, below Johnson. They had too much purpose in their talk to be artists about it. The endless eloquence of the Highgate days, to say nothing about the greater days before Highgate, was a powerful element in that revival of a spiritual or metaphysical, as opposed to a merely sensational, philosophy which has been going on ever since. No such results can be attributed to Johnson's talk. But talk is one thing and preaching another: and the final criticism on Coleridge as a talker was given once for all in Charles Lamb's well-known answer to his friend's question: " Did you ever hear me preach, Charles ? " " Never heard you do anything else." Luther again, though much more of a human being than Coleridge and apparently a livelier talker, was, after all, the leader of one of the greatest movements the world has ever seen, and like his disciple, Johnson's friend John Wesley, no doubt had no time to fold his legs, and have his talk out. Besides leaders of movements are necessarily somewhat narrow men. For them there is only one thing of importance in the world, and their talk inevitably lacks variety. That, on the other hand, is one of the three great qualities in which Johnson's talk is supreme. Without often aiming at being instructive it is not only nearly always interesting but with an amazing variety of interest. The theologian, the moral philosopher, the casuist, the scholar, the politician, the economist, the lawyer, the clergyman, the schoolmaster, the author, above all the amateur of life, all find in it abundance of food for their own particular tastes. Each of them—notably for instance, the political economist—may sometimes find Johnson mistaken; not one will ever find him dull. On every subject he has something to say which makes the reader's mind move faster than before, if it be but in disagreement. Reynolds, who had heard plenty of good talkers, thought no one could ever have exceeded Johnson in the capacity of talking well on any subject that came uppermost. His mere knowledge and information were prodigious. If a stranger heard him talk about leather he would imagine him to have been bred a tanner, or if about the school philosophy, he would suppose he had spent his life in the study of Scotus and Aquinas. No doubt the variety was a long way from universality. Johnson was too

human for the dulness of omniscience. He
had his dislikes as well as predilections. The
least affected of men, he particularly disliked
the then common fashion of dragging Greek
and Roman history into conversation. He
said that he " never desired to hear of the Punic
War while he lived," and when Fox talked
of Catiline he " thought of Tom Thumb." So
when Boswell used an illustration from Roman
manners he put him down with, " Why we
know very little about the Romans."

Wide as the country he could cover was,
he is always coming back to his favourite
topic, which can only be described as life;
how it is lived and how it ought to be; life
as a spectacle and life as a moral and social
problem. That by itself makes a sufficiently
varied field for talk. But real as his variety
was, it is still not the most remarkable thing
about his talk. Where he surpassed all men
was in the readiness with which he could put
what he possessed to use. Speaking of the
extraordinary quickness with which he " flew
upon " any argument, Boswell once said to
Sir Joshua, " he has no formal preparation,
no flourishing with the sword; he is through
your body in an instant." Sometimes he
condescended to achieve this by mere rudeness, as once when, being hard pressed in an
argument about the passions, he said, " Sir,

L

there is one passion I advise you to be careful
of. When you have drunk that glass don't
drink another." But the notion, which one
hears occasionally expressed, that his principal
argumentative weapon was rudeness is an
entire mistake. Every impartial reader of
Boswell will admit that the rudeness of his
retorts where it exists is entirely swallowed
up and forgotten in their aptness, ingenuity
and wit. He was rude sometimes, no doubt;
as, for instance, to the unfortunate young man
who went to him for advice as to whether he
should marry, and got for an answer, " Sir,
I would advise no man to marry who is not
likely to propagate understanding." But,
human nature being what it is, sympathy for
the victim is in such cases commonly extinguished in delighted admiration of the punishment. That will be still more whole-hearted
when the victim is obviously a bore, like the
gentleman who annoyed Johnson by persisting
in spite of discouragement in an argument
about the future life of brutes, till at last he
gave the fatal opportunity by asking, " with
a serious metaphysical pensive face," " But,
really, sir, when we see a very sensible dog,
we don't know what to think of him; " to
which Johnson, " rolling with joy at the
thought which beamed in his eye," replied,
" True, sir, and when we see a very foolish

fellow, we don't know what to think of *him*."
Conversation would be a weariness of the flesh
if one might never answer a fool according to
his folly : and such answers are not to be
called rude when the rudeness, if such there be,
is only one ingredient in a compound of which
the principal parts are humour and felicity.
And, of course, even this measure of rudeness
is only present occasionally, while the amazing
exactness of felicity seldom fails. Who does
not envy the readiness of mind which instantly provided him with the exact analogy
which he used to crush Boswell's plea for the
Methodist undergraduates expelled from
Oxford in 1768 ? "But was it not hard, sir,
to expel them, for I am told they were good
beings ?" "I believe they might be good
beings : but they were not fit to be in the
University of Oxford. A cow is a very good
animal in the field ; but we turn her out of a
garden." Note that, as usual with Johnson,
—and that is the astonishing thing—the
illustration, however far-fetched, is not merely
humorous but exactly to the point. Plenty
of men can compose such retorts at leisure :
the unique Johnsonian gift was that he had
them at his instant command. Or take one
other illustration ; a compliment this time,
and one of the swiftest as well as happiest
on record. Mrs. Siddons came to see him the

year before he died, and when she entered his room there was no chair for her. Another man would have been embarrassed by such a circumstance combined with such a visitor. Not so Johnson, who turned the difficulty into a triumph by simply saying with a smile, " Madam, you who so often occasion a want of seats to other people, will the more readily excuse the want of one yourself."

The third great quality of Johnson's talk is its style. His command of language was such as that he seems never to have been at a loss ; never to have fumbled, or hesitated, or fallen back upon the second best word ; he saw instantly the point he wanted to make, and was instantly ready with the best words in which to make it. It was said of him that all his talk could be written down and printed without a correction. That would, indeed, be double-edged praise to give to most men : but with Johnson it is absolutely true without being in the least damaging. For his talk is always talk, not writing or preaching ; and it is always his own. That dictum of Horace which he and Wilkes discussed at the famous dinner at Dilly's, *Difficile est proprie communia dicere*, gives the exact praise of Johnson as a talker. There are few things more difficult than to put the truths of common sense in

such a way as to make them your own. To do
so is one of the privileges of the masters of
style. Few people have had more of it than
Johnson. His prose, spoken or written, is
altogether wanting in some of the greatest
elements of style : it has no music, no mystery,
no gift of suggestion, very little of the higher
sort of imagination, nothing at all of what we
have been taught to call the Celtic side of the
English mind. But in this particular power
of making the old new, and the commonplace
individual, Johnson is among the great masters.
And he shows it in his talk even more than
in his writings. All that he says has that
supreme mark of style ; it cannot be translated
without loss. The only indisputable proof
of an author possessing style is his being un-
quotable except in his own words. If a
paraphrase will do he may have learning,
wisdom, profundity, what you will, but style
he has not. Style is the expression of an individual, appearing once and only once in the
world ; it is Keats or Carlyle or Swinburne : it
never has been and never will be anybody else.

Its presence in Johnson is painfully brought
home to any one who tries to quote his good
things without the assistance of a very
accurate verbal memory. Even when he
says such a thing as " This is wretched stuff,
sir," the words manage to have style because

they express his convictions in a way which is his, and no one else's. This is taking it at its lowest, of course; when we go a little further and take a sentence like the famous remark about Ossian, " Sir, a man might write such stuff for ever if he would abandon his mind to it," the sting in the word " abandon " is the sort of thing which other people devise at their desks, but which Johnson has ready on his lips for immediate use. So again, he seems to have been able not only to find the most telling word in a moment, but to put his thought in the most telling shape. Many people then and since disliked and disapproved of Bolingbroke. But has there ever, then or at any other time, been a man who could find such language for his disapproval as Johnson ? " Sir, he was a scoundrel and a coward : a scoundrel, for charging a blunderbuss against religion and morality : a coward, because he had not resolution to fire it off himself, but left half-a-crown to a beggarly Scotchman to draw the trigger after his death." It is at once as devastating as a volcano and as neat as a formal garden. So, in a smaller way, is his criticism of a smaller man. Dr. Adams, talking of Newton, Bishop of Bristol, whom Johnson disliked, once said, " I believe his *Dissertations on the Prophecies* is his great work," Johnson's instant answer was, " Why, sir, it is Tom's great work; but how far it is great, or how much of it is Tom's, are other questions." How mercilessly perfect! A thousand years of preparation could not have put it more shortly or more effectively. It both does the business in hand and gives expression to himself; nor is there in it a superfluous syllable; all of which is, again, another way of saying that it has style. And he did not need the stimulus of personal feeling to give him this energy of speech. The same gift is seen when he " *communia dicit*," when he is uttering some general reflection, the common wisdom of mankind. Molière said, " Je prends mon bien où je le trouve." Johnson might have used the same words with a slightly different meaning. He excelled all men in recoining the gold of common sense in his own mind. All the world has said " humanum est errare " : but the saying is newborn when Johnson clinches an argument with, " No, sir; a fallible being will fail somewhere." So on a hundred other commonplaces of discussion one may find him, all through Boswell's pages, adding that unanalysable something of himself in word or thought which makes the ancient dry bones stir again to life. " It is better to live rich than to die rich "; " no man is a hypocrite in his pleasures "; " it is the business of a wise man to be happy "; " he that runs against time has an antagonist not subject to casualties "; " the great excellence of a writer is to put into his book as much as his book will hold "; " there are few ways in which a man can be more innocently employed than in getting money "; " no woman is the worse for sense and knowledge "; but " supposing a wife to be of a studious or argumentative turn it would be very troublesome; for instance— if a woman should continually dwell upon the subject of the Arian heresy "; " a man should keep his friendship always in repair "; " to cultivate kindness is a valuable part of the business of life "; " every man is to take existence on the terms on which it is given to him "; " the man who talks to unburden his mind is the man to delight you "; " No, sir, let fanciful men do as they will, depend upon it it is difficult to disturb the system of life."

The man who thinks, as Taine thought, that sayings of this sort are mere commonplaces, will never understand Johnson : he may give up the attempt at once. The true commonplace is like the money of a spendthrift heir : his guineas come and go without his ever thinking for a moment where they came from or whither they go. But Johnson's commonplaces had been consciously earned and were

deliberately spent; he had made them himself,
and when he handed them on to others he
handed himself on with them.   Taine may
perhaps be excused; for it may require some
knowledge of English to be sure of detecting
the personal flavour Johnson gave to his
generalizations : but the Englishman who
misses it shows that he has mistaken the
ornaments of literature for its essence and
exposes himself to the same criticism as a man
who cannot recognize a genius unless he is
eccentric.   Johnson could break out in conversation as well as in his books into a noble
eloquence all his own; such a phrase as
" poisoning the sources of eternal truth,"
rises spontaneously to his lips when his
indignation is aroused.   His free language
disdained to be confined within any park
palings of pedantry.   Some of his most
characteristic utterances owe their flavour
to combining the language of the schools with
the language of the tavern : as when he said
of that strange inmate of his house, Miss
Carmichael, " Poll is a stupid slut.   I had
some hopes of her at first : but when I talked
to her tightly and closely I could make
nothing of her; she was wiggle waggle, and I
could never persuade her to be categorical."
He was the very antipodes of a retailer
of other men's thoughts in other men's words :

every chapter of Boswell brings its evidence of Johnsonian eloquence, of Johnsonian quaintness, raciness, and abundance, of the surprising flights of his fancy, of the inexhaustible ingenuity of his arguments and illustrations. No talk the world has ever heard is less like the talk of a commonplace man. Yet the supreme quality of it is not the ingenuity or the oddness or the wit : it is the thing Taine missed, the sovereign sanity of the Johnsonian common sense. Bagehot once said that it was the business of the English Prime Minister to have more common sense than any man. Johnson is the Prime Minister of literature; or perhaps, rather, of life. Not indeed for a time of revolution. For that we should have to go to some one less unwilling to " disturb the system of life." But for ordinary times, and in the vast majority of matters all times are ordinary, Johnson is the man. The Prime Minister is not the whole of the body politic, of course : and there are purposes for which we need people with more turn than Johnson for starting and pressing new ideas : but these will come best from below the gangway; and they will be none the worse in the end for having had to undergo the formidable criticism of a Prime Minister whose first article of faith is that the King's government must be carried on. The

slow-moving centrality of Johnson's mind, not
to be diverted by any far-looking whimsies
from the daily problem of how life was to be
lived, is not the least important of the qualities
that have given him his unique position in the
respect and affection of the English race.

CHAPTER V

JOHNSON'S WORKS

In his lifetime Johnson was chiefly thought
of as a great writer. To-day we think of him
chiefly as a great man. That is the measure
of Boswell's genius : no other biographer of
a great writer has unconsciously and unin-
tentionally thrown his hero's own works into
the shade. Scott will always have a hundred
times as many readers as Lockhart, and
Macaulay as Trevelyan. But in this, as in
some other ways, Boswell's involuntary greatness has upset the balance of truth. Johnson's writings are now much less read than
they deserve to be. For this there are a
variety of causes. Fourteen years before he
died, William Wordsworth was born at
Cockermouth; and fourteen years after his
death Wordsworth and Coleridge published
the volume which, more perhaps than any

other, started English literature on its great voyage into seas unsailed and unimagined by Johnson. The triumph of the Romantic movement inevitably brought with it the depreciation of the prophet of common sense in literature and in life. The great forces in the literature of the next seventy or eighty years were : in poetry, Wordsworth, Coleridge, Scott, Byron, Shelley, Keats; in prose, Scott, and then later on, Carlyle and Ruskin; every single one of them providing a wine by no means to be put into Johnsonian bottles.

Johnson, even more than other men in the eighteenth century, was abstract and general in his habit of mind and expression. The men of the new age were just the opposite; they were concrete and particular, lovers of detail and circumstance. The note of his writings had been common sense and rugged veracity; the dominant notes of theirs were picturesqueness, eloquence, emotion, even sentimentalism. Both the exaggerated hopes and the exaggerated fears aroused by the French Revolution disinclined their victims to listen to the middling sanity of Johnson. The hopes built themselves fancy castles of equality and fraternity which instinctively shrunk from the broadsides of Johnsonian ridicule. The fears hid themselves in caves of mediæval reaction and did not care to expose their eyes to the smarting daylight of Johnsonian common sense. His appeal had always been to argument : the new appeal was at worst to sentiment, at best to history for which Johnson was too true to his century to care anything. When Voltaire writes an article on monasticism, he has nothing to say about how it arose and developed; he neither knows nor cares anything about that. For him it is, like everything else, a thing to be judged in a court of abstract rationality, altogether independent of time and circumstance, and as such he has no difficulty in dismissing it with brilliant and witty contempt without telling us anything about what it actually is or was. It was this unhistorical spirit which, as Burke rightly preached, was the most fatal element in the French Revolution. But the French are not to be blamed alone for an intellectual atmosphere which was then universal in Europe. Little as Johnson would have liked the association, it must be admitted that he was in his way as pure and unhistorical a rationalist as Voltaire and the Encyclopædists; and that it was inevitable that the reaction in favour of history which Burke set in motion would tell against him as well as against them. Against the discovery that things can neither be rightly judged nor wisely reformed except by examining how they came to be what they

are, the whole eighteenth century, and in it
Johnson as well as Rousseau and Voltaire,
stands naked. And the abstract rationalizing
of that century was soon to have another
enemy in alliance with history, the new force
of science. Nothing has been more fatal to
the arbitrary despotism of mere reason than
the idea of development, of evolution. Directly
it is seen that all life exhibits itself in stages
it becomes obvious that the dry light of reason
will not provide the materials for true judgment until it has been coloured by a sym-
pathetic insight into the conditions of the
particular stage under discussion.

All these things, then, were against Johnson.
Alike to the new Liberalism ever more and
more drenched in sentiment, to the new
Conservatism ever more and more looking
for a base in history, to Romanticism in
literature with its stir, colour and emotion,
to science with its new studies and new
methods, the works of Johnson almost inevitably appeared as the dry bones of a dead
age. He had laughed at the Romans : and
behold the Romans had played a great part
in the greatest of Revolutions. He had
laughed at "noble prospects" and behold
the world was gone after them, and his,
"Who *can* like the Highlands ? " was drowned
in the poetry of Scott and Byron, and made

to appear narrow and vulgar in the presence
of Wordsworth. Only in one field did any
great change take place likely to be favourable
to Johnson's influence. The religious and
ecclesiastical revival which was so conspicuous
in England during the first half of the nineteenth century was naturally inclined to
exalt Johnson as the only strong Churchman,
and almost the only definite Christian among
the great writers of the eighteenth century.
The fact, too, that the most conspicuous centre
of the revival was Oxford, where Johnson's
name had always been affectionately remembered, helped to send its votaries back to him.
But this alliance could not be more than
partial. The Oxford Movement soon de-
generated into Mediævalism and Ritualism,
and no man was less fitted than Johnson to be
the prophet of either. The genius of common
sense was the very last leader their devotees
could wish for. And as the revival became
increasingly a reaction, relying more and more
on supposed precedent and less on the essential
reason of things, it inevitably got further away
from Johnson who cared everything for reason
and nothing at all for dubious history.

But it was not merely the changes that came
over the general mind of the nation that went
against Johnson ; it was still more the revolution in his own special branch of literature.

He was the last great English critic who treated poets, not as great men to be understood, but as school-boys to be corrected. He still applied, as the French have always done, a preordained standard to the work he was discussing, and declared it correct or not according to that test. The new criticism inaugurated by Coleridge aimed at interpretation rather than at magisterial regulation; and no one will now revert to the old. We never now find an English critic writing such notes, common till lately in France, as " cela n'est pas français," " cela ne se dit pas," " il faut écrire "—such and such a phrase, and not the phrase used by the poet receiving chastisement. But Johnson does conclude his plays of Shakespeare with such remarks as : "The conduct of this play is deficient." " The passions are directed to their true end." " In this play are some passages which ought not to have been exhibited, as we are told they were, to a maiden Queen." The substance of these comments may often be just, but for us their tone is altogether wrong. We no longer think that a critic, even if he be Johnson, should distribute praise or blame to poets, even of much less importance than Shakespeare, with the confident assurance of a school-master looking over a boy's exercise. Johnson's manner, then, as a critic was against him with the nineteenth century. But so also was his matter. The poetry he really believed in was that of what the nineteenth century came to regard as the age of prose. Of his three great *Lives* we feel that those of Dryden and Pope express the pleasure he spontaneously and unconsciously felt, while that of Milton is a reluctant tribute extorted from him by a genius he could not resist. Among the few poets in his long list for whom the nineteenth century cared much are Gray and Collins : and of Collins he says almost nothing in the way of admiration, and of Gray very little. Even when he wrote of Shakespeare, to whom he paid a tribute that will long outlive those of blind idolatry, what he praised is not what seemed greatest to the lovers of poetry in the next generation. A critic who found " no nice discriminations of character in Macbeth," and defended Tate's " happy family " ending of Lear, was not unnaturally dismissed or ignored by those who had sat at the feet of Coleridge or Lamb.

There is still one other thing which told against him. No one influenced the course of English literature in the nineteenth century so much as Wordsworth. And Wordsworth was a determined reformer not only of the matter of poetry but of its very language.

M

He overstated his demands and did not get his ideas clear to his own mind, as may be seen by the fact that he instinctively recoiled from applying the whole of them in his own poetical practice. But he plainly advocated two things as essential parts of his reform; poetry was to go back for its subject to the primary universal facts of human life, and it was to use as far as possible the language actually used by plain men in speaking to each other. Both these demands had to submit to modification; but both profoundly influenced the subsequent development of English poetry : and both were, as Wordsworth knew, opposed to the teaching and practice of Johnson. The return to simplicity involved a preference for such poetry as Percy's Ballads which Johnson had ridiculed, and a distaste for the poetry of the town which Johnson admired. And both in the famous *Preface* and in the *Appendix* and *Essay Supplementary* added to it Wordsworth refers to Johnson and seems to recognize him as the most dangerous authority with whom he has to contend. In that contest Wordsworth was on the whole decidedly victorious; and to that extent again Johnson was discredited. Nor was it the language of poetry only which was affected. Under the influences which Wordsworth, Scott and Byron set

moving, the old colourless, abstract, professedly
classical language was supplanted even in
prose. The new prose was enriched by a
hundred qualities of music, colour and suggestion, at which the prose of the eighteenth
century had never aimed. Those who had
enjoyed the easy grace of Lamb, the swift
lightnings of Carlyle, the eloquence, playful-
ness and tenderness of Ruskin, the lucid
suavity of Newman, were sure to conclude
in their haste that the prose of Johnson was
a thing pompous, empty and dull.

But against all these indictments a reaction
has now begun. Like other reactions its first
utterances are apt to be extravagant. In
literature as in politics those who at last take
their courage in their hands and defy the
established opinion are obliged to shout to
keep their spirits up. So Sir Walter Raleigh,
whose *Six Essays* at once put the position of
Johnson on a new footing, has allowed himself
to say of some sentences from *The Rambler*
that they are " prose which will not suffer
much by comparison with the best in the
language." But, apart from these inevitable
over-statements of defiance, what he has said
about Johnson is unanswered and unanswerable. And at last it is able to fall upon a
soil prepared for it. In all directions the
Gothic movement, which was so inevitably

unfavourable to the fame of Johnson, has crumbled and collapsed. A counter movement seems to be in progress. The classical revival in architecture is extending into other fields and though no one wishes to undo the poetic achievement of the nineteenth century, every one has come to wish to understand that of the eighteenth. We shall never again think that Dryden and Pope had the essence of poetry in them to the same extent, as, for instance, Wordsworth or Shelley; but neither shall we ever again treat them with the superficial and ignorant contempt which was not uncommon twenty or thirty years ago. The twentieth century is not so confident as its predecessor that the poetry and criticism of the eighteenth may safely be ignored.

If, then, we are not to ignore Johnson's writing, what are we to remember ? In a sketch like this the point of view to be taken is that of the man with a general interest in English letters, not that of the specialist in the eighteenth century, or indeed, that of any specialist at all. Well, then, first of all Johnson wrote verses which though not great poetry have some fine qualities. They are, like so much of the verse of that century, chiefly " good sense put into good metre." That is what Twining, the Aristotelian critic, said of them when Johnson died. He had a much finer sense of poetry than Johnson, and he was perfectly right in this criticism. But it is a loss and not a gain that, since Wordsworth gave us such a high conception of what poetry should be, we have ceased to take pleasure in good verses simply for their own sake. In the eighteenth century a new volume of verse became at once the talk of the town and every cultivated person read it. Now we have allowed poetry to become a thing so esoteric in its exaltation that only the poetically minded can read it. Neither the *Excursion* nor the *Epipsychidion* could possibly be read by the great public. All the world could and did read Pope's *Epistles* and Goldsmith's *Traveller*. It may have been worth while to pay the price for the new greatness of poetry that came in with the nineteenth century; but it is at any rate right to remember that there was a price, and that it has had to be paid. It may be that some day we shall be able again to take pleasure in well-turned verses without losing our appreciation of higher things. Good verse is, really, a delightful thing even when it is not great poetry, and we are too apt now-a-days to forget that verse has one great inherent advantage over prose, that it impresses itself on the memory as no prose can. We can all quote scores of lines from Pope, though we may not know who it is whom we are quoting. That is the pleasure of art. And if the lines, as often, utter the voice of good sense in morals or politics, it is its accidental utility also. Johnson has, of course, little of Pope's amazing dexterity, wit and finish. But he has some qualities of which Pope had nothing or not very much. In his verse, as everywhere else, he shows a sense of the real issues of things quite out of the reach of a well-to-do wit living in his library, like Pope; what he writes may be in form an imitation of Juvenal, but it is in essence a picture of life and often of his own life.

How large a part of the business of poetry consists in giving new expression to the old truths of experience, is known to all the great poets and seen in their practice. Johnson can do this with a force that refuses to be forgotten.

" But few there are whom hours like these await,
Who set unclouded in the gulfs of fate.
From Lydia's monarch should the search descend,
By Solon cautioned to regard his end,
In life's last scene what prodigies surprise,
Fears of the brave and follies of the wise !
From Marlborough's eyes the streams of dotage flow,
And Swift expires a driveller and a show."

Such lines almost challenge Pope on his own

ground, meeting his rapier-like dexterity of neatness with heavy sword-strokes of sincerity and strength. But here, as in the prose, the true Johnsonian excellence is best seen when he is in the confessional.

" Should no disease thy torpid veins invade,
  Nor Melancholv's phantoms haunt thy
      shade;
Yet hope not life from grief or danger free,
Nor think the doom of man reversed for thee—
Deign on the passing world to turn thine eyes,
And pause awhile from Letters to be wise;
There mark what ills the scholar's life assail,
Toil, envy, want, the patron, and the gaol."

There, and in such lines as the stanza on Levett—

" His virtues walked their narrow round,
  Nor made a pause, nor left a void;
And sure the Eternal Master found
  The single talent well employed,"

one hears the authentic unique voice of Johnson; not that of a great poet but of a real man to whom it is always worth while to listen, and not least when he puts his thoughts into the pointed shape of verse.

Still, of course, prose and not verse is his natural medium. And here a word should be said about that prose style of his which had an immense vogue for a time and plainly

influenced most of the writers of his own and
the following generation, even men so great
as Gibbon and the young Ruskin, and women
so brilliant as Fanny Burney. Then a reaction came and it was generally denounced
as pompous, empty and verbose. After the
Revolution people gave up wearing wigs, and
with the passing of wigs and buckle-shoes
there came a dislike of the dignified deportment of the eighteenth century in weightier
matters than costume. Now Johnson, whatever he did at other times, was commonly inclined to put on his wig before he took up his
pen. His elaborate and antithetical phrases
are apt to go into pairs like people in a Court
procession, and seem at first sight to belong
altogether to what we should call an artificial
as well as a ceremonious age. His style is the
exact opposite of Dryden's, of which he said
that, having "no prominent or discriminative
characters," it " could not easily be imitated
either seriously or ludicrously." Johnson's
could be, and often was, imitated in both
spirits. Even in his lifetime, when it was
most admired, it was already parodied. Goldsmith was talking once of the art of writing
fables, and of the necessity, if your fable be
about " little fishes," of making them talk
like " little fishes "; Johnson laughed : upon
which Goldsmith said, " Why, Dr. Johnson,

this is not so easy as you seem to think : for
if you were to make little fishes talk, they would
talk like whales." That was the weak spot
in Johnson on which the wits and critics
seized at once : there is a good deal of mis-
placed magniloquence in his writings. When
the sage in *Rasselas* says, " I have missed the
endearing elegance of female friendship, and
the happy commerce of domestic tenderness,"
we now feel at once that the simple and natural
thought gains nothing and loses much by this
heavy pomp of abstract eloquence. So when
Johnson wants to say in the eleventh *Idler* that
it is wrong and absurd to let our spirits depend
on the weather, he makes his reader laugh
or yawn, rather than listen, by the ill-timed
elaboration of his phrases : " to call upon the
sun for peace and gaiety, or deprecate the
clouds lest sorrow should overwhelm us, is the
cowardice of idleness, and the idolatry of folly."
So much must be admitted. Johnson is often
turgid and pompous, often grandiose with an
artificial and undesired grandiloquence. No
one, however, who has read his prose works
will pretend that this is a fair account of his
ordinary style. You may read many *Ramblers* in succession and scarcely find a marked
instance of it; and, as every one knows, his
last, longest and pleasantest work, the *Lives of
the Poets*, is almost free from it. All through

his life one can trace a kind of progress as he gradually shakes off these mannerisms, and writes as easily as he talked. They are most conspicuous in *The Rambler* and *Rasselas*. But even there, through all the heaviness, born perhaps of the too obvious desire to instruct and improve, we get more than occasional suggestions of the trenchant force which we most associate with the pages of Boswell.

" My curiosity," said Rasselas, " does not very strongly lead me to survey piles of stone, or mounds of earth; my business is with man. I came hither not to measure fragments of temples, or trace choaked aqueducts, but to look upon the various scenes of the present world. . . . To judge rightly of the present we must oppose it to the past; for all judgment is comparative, and of the future nothing can be known."

There is nothing here of the intimacy and charm which, as Dryden and Cowley had already shown, and Johnson himself was occasionally to show in his last years, a plain prose may possess; but of the lucidity and force which are its most necessary characteristics never prose exhibited more. Those who know their Boswell will catch in the passage a pleasant foretaste of the outburst to Thrale when he wanted Johnson to contrast

French and English scenery: "Never heed such nonsense, sir; a blade of grass is always a blade of grass, whether in one country or another; let us, if we *do* talk, talk about something; men and women are my subjects of inquiry: let us see how these differ from those we have left behind."

This natural trenchancy gets freer play, of course, in the talk than in the writings. But it is in them all from the first, even in *Rasselas*, even in *The Rambler*. "The same actions performed by different hands produce different effects, and, instead of rating the man by his performances we rate too frequently the performances by the man. . . . Benefits which are received as gifts from wealth are exacted as debts from indigence; and he that in a high station is celebrated for superfluous goodness would in a meaner condition have barely been confessed to have done his duty."

It is not necessary to multiply citations. What is found even in *The Rambler*, which he himself in later years found "too wordy," is found much more abundantly in the Dictionary and the *Shakespeare;* and as he grows old, and, with age and authority, increasingly indifferent to criticism and increasingly confident in his own judgment, there gradually comes an ease and familiarity which without diminishing the perfect lucidity of the phrases adds sometimes to the old contemptuous force, and occasionally brings a new intimacy and indulgence. The writing becomes gradually more like the talk. Nobody in his earlier work was ever quite so unceremoniously kicked downstairs as Wilkes was in *The False Alarm*.

"All wrong ought to be rectified. If Mr. Wilkes is deprived of a lawful seat, both he and his electors have reason to complain, but it will not be easily found why, among the innumerable wrongs of which a great part of mankind are hourly complaining, the whole care of the publick should be transferred to Mr. Wilkes and the freeholders of Middlesex, who might all sink into non-existence without any other effect than that there would be room made for a new rabble and a new retailer of sedition and obscenity."

This is the old power of invective indulged now with the reckless indifference of a man who is talking among friends, knows his power and enjoys using it. But the ease of his later manner more commonly takes the form of a redoubled directness in his old appeal to universal experience, or that of those natural indulgences of old age, anecdote and autobiography. Take, for instance, the first volume of his *Lives*. It is not only full of such admirable generalizations as that in which he sums up the case for a literary as against a mathematical or scientific education : " The truth is that the knowledge of external nature and the sciences which that knowledge requires or includes are not the great or the frequent business of the human mind. . . . We are perpetually moralists : we are geometricians only by chance "; or that in which he expresses his contempt for Dryden exchanging Billingsgate with Settle : " Minds are not levelled in their powers, but when they are first levelled in their desires "; or the pregnant commonplace with which he prefaces his derision of the artificial love-poems which Cowley thought it necessary to address to an imaginary mistress : " It is surely not difficult, in the solitude of a college or in the bustle of the world, to find useful studies and serious employment." This is the Johnson his readers had known from the beginning. What is newer are the personal touches sprinkled all over the book. Here he will bring in a fact about his friend, Sir Joshua Reynolds; there he will give a piece of information derived from " my father, an old bookseller." He who studied life and manners before all things loves to record the personal habits of his poets and to try their writings rather by the tests of life than of criticism. He was, perhaps, the first great critic to take the seeming trifles of daily life out of the hands of gossips and anecdote-mongers, and give them their due place in the study of a great man. All this necessarily gave him something of the colloquial ease of the writer of recollections. Nothing could be simpler than his style when he tells us of Milton that " when he first rose he heard a chapter in the Hebrew Bible and then studied till twelve; then took some exercise for an hour; then dined; then played on the organ, and sang, or heard another sing; then studied to six; then entertained his visitors till eight; then supped, and after a pipe of tobacco and a glass of water went to bed." On which his comment is characteristic and plainly autobiographical. " So is his life described; but this even tenour appears attainable only in colleges. He that lives in the world will sometimes have the succession of his practice broken and confused. Visitors, of whom Milton is represented to have had great numbers, will come and stay unseasonably : business, of which every man has some, must be done when others will do it." This may still have about it something of the style of a school-master, but of a school-master who teaches the art of living, not without having learnt by experience the difficulty of practising it.

So we may trace the gradual diminution, but never the entire disappearance, of the excessive " deportment " which is the best known feature of Johnson's style. Of another feature often found in it by hostile critics less need be said because it is not really there at all. Johnson is frequently accused of verbosity. If that word means merely pomposity it has already been discussed. If it means, as it should mean, the use of superfluous words adding nothing to the sense, few authors are so seldom guilty of it as Johnson. There are many good writers, Scott, for instance, and the authors of the Book of Common Prayer, in whom a hurried reader might frequently omit half a phrase without depriving his hearers of an ounce of meaning. But you cannot do that with Johnson. Words that add neither information nor argument to what has gone before are exceptionally rare in him. Take his style at its worst. " It is therefore to me a severe aggravation of a calamity, when it is such as in the common opinion will not justify the acerbity of exclamation, or support the solemnity of vocal grief." Heavier writing there could scarcely be. But every word has its duty to do. The supposed speaker has been saying that he is, like Sancho Panza, quite unable to suffer in silence; and he adds that this makes many a misfortune harder for him to bear than it need be : for it may arise from an injury which other people think too trifling to justify any open expression of anger, or from an accident that may seem to them so petty that they will not endure any serious lamentation about it. Johnson's way of saying this is pompous and rather absurd; but it is not verbose. So when he says that he knows nothing of Mallet except " what is supplied by the unauthorized loquacity of common fame," it is possible to dislike the phrase; it is not possible to deny that the words are as full of meaning as words can be.

The fact is that Johnson's style has the merits and defects of scholarship. He knows, as a scholar will, how every word came upon the paper, consequently he seldom uses language which is either empty or inexact; but with the scholar's accuracy he has also the scholar's pride. The dignity of literature was constantly in his mind as he wrote; and he did not always write the better for it. Books in his day and in his eyes were still rather solemn things to be kept above the linguistic level of conversation. Dryden and Addison had already begun to make the great discovery that the best prose style has no conscious air of literature about it; but the new doctrine had not reached the mass either of writers or readers. And it never completely reached Johnson. He himself once accidentally gave one of the best definitions of the new style when he said of Shakespeare's comic dialogue that it was gathered from that kind of conversation which is "above grossness and below refinement." And at the end of his life he even occasionally produced some good specimens of it. But, taking his work as a whole, it must be admitted that he could rarely bring himself to be "below refinement," the refinement not of the drawing-room but of the library. In what he says he is always a man; in the way he says it he is nearly always too visibly an author. Those who have eyes to see and the will to look never fail of finding the man; but the author stares them in the face.

His prose works may be divided into two classes, those in which he is primarily a moralist, and those in which he is primarily a critic. Life and manners are never out of his mind; but while they are the direct and avowed subject of *The Rambler*, *The Idler* and *Rasselas*, they only come, as it were, indirectly into the *Dictionary*, the *Shakespeare* and the *Lives of the Poets*, where the ostensible business is the criticism of literature. Outside these categories are the political pamphlets, the interesting *Journey to the Western Islands*,

N

and a great quantity of miscellaneous literary hack-work. All of these have mind and character in them, or they would not be Johnson's; but they call for no special discussion. Nor do the *Prayers and Meditations*, which of course he did not publish himself. It is enough to say that, while fools have frequently ridiculed them, all who have ever realized that there is such a thing as the warfare of the spirit with its own weakness, will find a poignant interest in the tragedy of Johnson's inner life, always returning again and again to the battle in which he seemed to himself to be always defeated.

The Rambler, *The Idler* and *Rasselas* fill four volumes out of the twelve in the 1823 library edition of Johnson. When Johnson decided to bring out a periodical paper he, of course, had the model of the *Spectator* and *Tatler* before him. But he had in him less of the graces of life than Addison and Steele, and a far deeper sense of the gravity of its issues; with the result that *The Rambler* and *The Idler* are much heavier than their predecessors, not only in style but in substance. They deal much more avowedly with instruction. As we read them we wonder, not at the slow sale of the original papers, but at the editions which the author lived to see. We stand amazed to-day at the audacity of a journalist who dares to offer, and at the patience or wisdom of a public which is content twice a week to read, not exciting events or entertaining personalities, but sober essays on the most ancient and apparently threadbare of topics. Here are Johnson's subjects for the ten *Ramblers* which appeared between November 20 and December 22, 1750 : the shortness of life, the value of good-humour, the folly of heirs who live on their expectations, peevishness, the impossibility of knowing mankind till one has experienced misfortune, the self-deceptions of conscience, the moral responsibilities of men of genius, the power of novelty, the justice of suspecting the suspicious, the pleasures of change and in particular that of winter following upon summer. None of these can be called exciting topics. Yet when there is a man of real power to discuss them, and men of sense to listen to him, they can make up a book which goes through many editions, is translated into foreign languages, and is called by a great critic a hundred and fifty years after its appearance, a " splendid repository of wisdom and truth." With the exception of the first word, Sir Walter Raleigh's daring praise may be accepted as strictly true. There is nothing splendid about *The Rambler* or *The Idler*. The more shining qualities of literature, except occasional eloquence, are conspicuously wanting in them. There is no imagination, little of the fancy, wit and readiness of illustration so omnipresent in Johnson's talk, little power of drawing character, very little humour. He often puts his essay into the form of a story, but it remains an essay still. His strength is always in the reflections, never in the facts related or the persons described. The club of Essex gentlemen who fancied themselves to be satirized in *The Rambler* were only an extreme instance of the common vanity which loves to fancy itself the subject of other people's thoughts. Johnson's portraits have not life enough to be caricatures; still less can posterity find in them the finer truth of human beings. His was a profounder mind than Addison's; but he could not have drawn Sir Roger de Coverley. He had not "run about the world," as he said, for nothing, and he knew a great deal about men and women; but he could not create. *Rasselas*, his only professed story, is a total failure as a story. It is a series of moral essays, and whoever reads it must read it for the same reasons as he reads *The Rambler*. The remark Johnson absurdly made of Richardson's masterpiece is exactly true of his own *Rasselas :* " If you were to read it for the story your impatience would be so fretted that you would hang yourself."

In all these things, as elsewhere, his strength lies in shrewdness, in a common sense that has been through the fire of experience, in a real love of wisdom and truth. There is a story that Charlotte Brontë, when a girl of sixteen, broke out very angrily at some one who said she was always talking about clever men such as Johnson and Sheridan. "Now you don't know the meaning of clever," she said; "Sheridan might be clever—scamps often are, but Johnson hadn't a spark of 'cleverality' in him." That remark gives the essence of *The Rambler*. Whoever wants "cleverality," whoever wants what Mr. Shaw and Mr. Chesterton supply so brilliantly and abundantly to the present generation, had best leave Johnson alone. The signal merit of his writings is the exact opposite of "cleverality"; it is that he always means exactly what he says. He often talked for victory, but except, perhaps, in the political pamphlets he always wrote for truth.

Books like *The Rambler* and *Rasselas* do not easily lend themselves to illustration; the effect they produce is a cumulative effect. Slowly, as we read paper after paper, the mind and character of Johnson take hold of us; what we began with impatience or perhaps with contempt, we put down with respect and admiration. At the end we feel that we would gladly put our lives into the hands of this rough, wise, human, limited, lovable man. To get to that impression the books must be read; but one or two illustrations may be given. There is nothing new to say about death, but the human heart will itself be dead when it is willing to give up saying again the old things that have been said on that subject from the beginning of the world. Who puts more of it into saying them than Johnson?

"When a friend is carried to his grave, we at once find excuses for every weakness, and palliations of every fault; we recollect a thousand endearments which before glided off our minds without impression, a thousand favours unrepaid, a thousand duties unperformed, and wish, vainly wish, for his return, not so much that we may receive, as that we may bestow happiness, and recompense that kindness which before we never understood."

Where in this is the pompous pedant who is so commonly supposed to be the writer of Johnson's books? The English language has not often been more beautifully handled. It is true that, until one looks closely, the last words of the first sentence appear to be a piece of empty verbiage; but taken as a whole the passage moves with a grave music fitted to its sober truth. The art in it is as admirable as the emotion is sincere.

Or take a different illustration from a *Rambler*, in which he is discussing the well-known fact that the commonest cause of shyness is self-importance.

"Those who are oppressed by their own reputation will perhaps not be comforted by hearing that their cares are unnecessary. But the truth is that no man is much regarded by the rest of the world. He that considers how little he dwells upon the condition of others will learn how little the attention of others is attracted by himself. While we see multitudes passing before us of whom, perhaps, not one appears to deserve our notice or excite our sympathy, we should remember that we, likewise, are lost in the same throng; that the eye which happens to glance upon us is turned in a moment on him that follows us, and that the utmost which we can reasonably hope or fear is to fill a vacant hour with prattle, and be forgotten."

All good writers write of themselves; not, as vain people talk, of their triumphs and grievances and diseases, but of what they have succeeded in grasping as their own out of all the floating wisdom of the world. In a passage like this one almost hears Johnson reflecting aloud as he walks back in his old age to his lonely rooms after an evening at "The Club" or the Mitre. It is the graver side of what he once said humorously to Boswell : " I may leave this town and go to Grand Cairo without being missed here or observed there." But the autobiographical note is sometimes even plainer. Of whom could he be thinking so much as of himself when he wrote the 101st *Rambler* ?

" Perhaps no kind of superiority is more flattering or alluring than that which is conferred by the powers of conversation, by extemporaneous sprightliness of fancy, copiousness of language, and fertility of sentiment. In other exertions of genius, the greater part of the praise is unknown and unenjoyed ; the writer, indeed, spreads his reputation to a wider extent, but receives little pleasure or advantage from the diffusion of his name, and only obtains a kind of nominal sovereignty over regions which pay no tribute. The colloquial wit has always his own radiance reflected on himself, and enjoys all the pleasure which he bestows ; he finds his power confessed by every one that approaches him, sees friendship kindling with rapture and attention swelling into praise."

In that shrewd observation lies the secret

of the comparative unproductiveness of his later years. Men like Dryden and Gibbon and Lecky are the men to get through immense literary labours : to a great talker like Johnson what can the praises of reviewers or of posterity be in comparison with the flashing eyes, and attentive ears, the expectant silence and spontaneous applause, of the friends in whom he has an immediate mirror of his success ?

It is impossible and unnecessary to multiply illustrations. The only thing that need be added is that even in *Rasselas* and the essays, Johnson's slow-moving style is constantly relieved by those brief and pregnant generalizations of which he is one of the greatest masters in our language. They are so close to life as all men know it, that the careless reader, as we have already seen, is apt to take them for platitudes; but there is all the difference between the stale superficiality which coldly repeats what only its ears have heard, and these sayings of Johnson heated to new energy in the fires of conscience, thought and experience. "I have already enjoyed too much," says the Prince in *Rasselas ;* "give me something to desire." And then, a little later, as so often happens with the wise, comes the other side of the medal of truth : " Human life is everywhere a state in which much is to be endured and little to be enjoyed." Or take such sentences as that embodying the favourite Johnsonian and Socratic distinction : " to man is permitted the contemplation of the skies, but the practice of virtue is commanded "; or, " we will not endeavour to fix the destiny of kingdoms : it is our business to consider what beings like us may perform "; or such sayings as, " the truth is that no mind is much employed upon the present : recollection and anticipation fill up almost all our moments "; " marriage has many pains but celibacy has no pleasures "; " envy is almost the only vice which is practicable at all times and in every place "; " no place affords a more striking conviction of the vanity of human hopes than a public library "; " I have always thought it the duty of an anonymous author to write as if he expected to be hereafter known "; or, last of all, to bring citation to an end, that characteristic saying about the omnipresence of the temptations of idleness : " to do nothing is in every man's power : we can never want an opportunity of omitting duties."

Johnson's principal work as a scholar and critic of literature is to be found in his Dictionary, the edition of Shakespeare, and the *Lives of the Poets*. It has the strength and weakness which might be anticipated by any intelligent person who had read Boswell and the *Ramblers*. It abounds in manliness, courage, and modesty : it never for an instant forgets that literature exists for the sake of life and not life for the sake of literature : it has no esoteric or professional affectations, but says plain things in plain words such as all can understand. The literary critic can have no more valuable qualities than these. But they do not complete his equipment. The criticism of Johnson has many limitations. He was entirely without æsthetic capacity. Not only were music and the plastic arts nothing to him—as indeed they have been to many good judges of poetry—but he does not appear to have possessed any musical ear or much power of imagination. It is not going too far to say that of the highest possibilition of poetry he had no conception. He imagines he has disposed of *Lycidas* by exhibiting its " inherent improbability " in the eyes of a crude common sense : a triumph which is as easy and as futile as his refutation of Berkeley's metaphysics by striking his foot upon the ground. The truth is of course that in each case he is beating the air. The stamp upon the ground would have been a triumphant answer to a fool who should say that the senses cannot feel : it does not touch

Berkeley who says they cannot know. So the attack on *Lycidas* might be fatal to a judge who put his judgment into the form of a pastoral; as the criticism of a poet it is in the main simply irrelevant. It is evident that what Johnson admires in Milton is the power of his mind and the elevation of his character, not at all his purely poetic gifts. He never betrays the slightest suspicion that in speaking of Milton he is speaking of one of the very greatest artists the world has ever known. He thought blank verse was verse only to the eye, and found the " numbers " of *Lycidas* " unpleasing." He did not believe that anybody read *Paradise Lost* for pleasure, and said so with his usual honesty. He saw nothing in *Samson Agonistes* but the weakness of the plot; of the heights and depths of its poetry he perceived nothing. He preferred the comedies to the tragedies of Shakespeare : felt the poet in him much less than the omniscient observer of universal life : and indeed, if we may judge by what he says in the preface to the Dictionary, hardly thought of him as a master of poetic language at all. He had evidently no appreciation of the Greek dramatists. The thing that moves him in poetry is eloquence of expression and energy of thought : both good things but things that can exist outside poetry. The arguments in which he states his objections to devotional poetry in the life of Waller show that he regarded poetry as an artful intellectual embroidery, not as the only fit utterance of an exalted mood.

To such a conception we can never return after all that has been done for us by Wordsworth and Coleridge and Matthew Arnold, to say nothing of some living critics like Mr. Yeats. No one who cares at all for poetry now could think of regretting an unwritten epic in the language Johnson uses about Dryden's: "it would doubtless have improved our numbers and enlarged our language; and might perhaps have contributed by pleasing instruction to rectify our opinions and purify our manners." It is not that such criticism is false but that it is beside the mark. An epic poem may do all these things, as a statesman may play golf or act as churchwarden : but when he dies it is not his golf or his churchwardenship that we feel the loss of. Put this remark of Johnson's by the side of such sayings as have now become the commonplaces of criticism. We need not go out to look for them. They are everywhere, in the mouths of all who speak of poetry. One opens Keats' letters at random and finds him saying, " Poetry should be great and unobtrusive, a thing that enters

into one's soul." One takes up the work of a
living critic, Mr. Eccles, and one finds him saying, in his book on French poetry, that when
we go to the very root of poetry one of the
things we discern is the " mystical collabora-
tion of a consecrated element of form in the
travail of the spirit." Language of this sort
is now almost the ordinary language of
criticism. Blake and Wordsworth did not
conquer the kingdom of criticism in a moment
or a year : but when at last they did its whole
tone and attitude necessarily changed. Where
Johnson, even while praising Milton's " skill
in harmony " as " not less than his learning,"
discusses it merely as " skill," as a sort of
artisanship, and misses all its subtler and
rarer mysteries, we see in it an inspiration
as much an art, life itself raised as it were
to a higher denomination, a power of spirit—

" Dead things with inbreathed sense able to
    pierce."

It is the measure of the distance we have
travelled away from Johnson that even plain
people to-day, if they care for poetry at all,
find much more in it than a piece of cunning
craftsmanship. It is always that no doubt :
but for us to-day it is also something far
higher : a symbol of eternity. And more
than a symbol, a sacrament : for it not only

suggests but reveals : it *is* the truth which
it signifies; itself a part, as all those who
have ever profoundly felt its influence are
assured, of the eternal order of things to
which it points.

Plainly, then, some of the things which
now seem to us to be of the very innermost
essence of poetry are not things which can
be weighed in any scales known to Johnson.
Yet in spite of his limitations he is certainly
one of the masters of English criticism. The
great critic may be said to be one who leaves
the subject-matter of his criticism more
respected and better understood than he found
it. Johnson's principal subjects were the
English language, the plays of Shakespeare,
and the poets from Cowley to his own day.
There can be no question of the services he
rendered to the English language. His
Dictionary, as was inevitable, had many
faults, especially of etymology : but its
publication marks an epoch in the history of
English. It was a kind of challenge to the
world. Other nations had till then inclined
to look upon our language and literature as
barbarous : and we had not been very sure
ourselves that we had any right to a place on
the Parnassus of the nations. Great men
in Italy and France had thought those

languages worth the labours of a lifetime.
In England before Johnson's Dictionary,
nothing had been done to claim for English
an equal place with Italian or French in the
future of the literature and civilization of the
world. What companies of learned men had
taken generations to do for foreign countries
had now been done for England in a few years
by the industry, and abilities of a single
scholar. Englishmen who took a pride in
their language might now do so with understanding : foreigners who wished to learn
English could now learn in the method and
spirit of a scholar, no longer merely as travellers or tradesmen. The two folio volumes of
the Dictionary were the visible evidence that
English had taken its place in the literary
polity of Europe. They were the fit pre-
cursors of the triumphant progress soon to be
made by Burke and Scott and Byron. The
other great service which Johnson rendered to
our language by his Dictionary and its Preface
could only have been rendered by a man so
superior to the narrowness of scholarship as
Johnson. No doubt as a single individual
in a private position he was not exposed to
such temptations to law-giving arrogance as
the French Academicians. But nevertheless
it is to his credit that he frankly recognized
that a language is a living thing, and that

life means growth and growth change. So far as it lay in the power of the French critics the new dignity that came to their language in the seventeenth century was made to involve a pedantic and sterile immobility. The meaning, the spelling, the arrangement, of words was to be regulated by immutable law, and all who disobeyed were to be punished as lawless and insolent rebels. Johnson knew better. Both his melancholy and his common sense taught him that "language is the work of man, of a being from whom permanence and stability cannot be derived." He knew that words coming from human mouths must follow the law of life : "when they are not gaining strength they are losing it." His business was not the vain folly of trying to bind the future in fetters : it was to record the present use and past history of words as accurately as he could ascertain them, and, by showing Englishmen what their heritage was and whence they had received it, to make them proud of its past and jealous of its future. The pedant wishes to apply a code of Median rigidity to correct the barbarous freedom of a language to which scholarship has never applied itself. Johnson gave our savages laws and made them citizens of a constitutional state : but, however venerable the laws and however little to be

o

changed without grave reason, he knew that, if the literary polity of England lived and grew, new needs would arise, old customs become obsolete, and the laws of language, like all others, would have to be changed to meet the new conditions. But the urgent business at that moment was to codify the floating and uncertain rules which a student of English found it difficult to collect and impossible to reconcile. Johnson might often be wrong : but after him there was at least an authority to appeal to : and that, as he himself felt, was a great step forward : for it is of more importance that the law should be known than that it should be right.

To have done all this, and to have explained what was done and what was attempted in language of such manliness, modesty and eloquence as that of the great Preface, is to have rendered one of the greatest services that can be rendered to the literature of a nation. " The chief glory of every people," says Johnson, " arises from its authors." That would be a bold thing to say to-day and was a bolder then, especially in so prosaic a place as the preface to a dictionary. But the world sees its truth more and more. And it is less out of place in a dictionary than appears at first sight. For that glory is not easily gained or recognized till both authors

and people realize that their language is the
peer of the greatest in the world, a fit vehicle
for the highest thoughts that can enter the
mind of man. And towards that result in
England only a few works of genius have
contributed more than Johnson's Dictionary.

After the language itself comes the most
priceless of its monuments. The services
Johnson rendered to Shakespeare are only
second to those he rendered to the language
in which Shakespeare wrote. The Preface
to his edition of Shakespeare is certainly the
most masterly piece of his literary criticism :
and it may still be doubted, after all that has
been written about Shakespeare in the century
and a half that separate it from our own day,
whether the world can yet show any sixty
pages about Shakespeare exhibiting so much
truth and wisdom as these. All Johnson's
gifts are seen at their best in it : the lucidity,
the virile energy, the individuality of his
style : the unique power of first placing himself
on the level of the plain man and then lifting
the plain man to his : the resolute insistence
on life and reason, not learning or ingenuity,
as the standard by which books are to be
judged. No one ever was so free as Johnson
from that pest of literature which a fine
French critic, one of the subtlest of his
countrymen, called " l'ingénieux sans bon

O 2

sens "; and he never showed himself so free
of it as in his Shakespeare. The master of
life who " whether life or nature be his subject,
shows plainly that he has seen with his own
eyes," inspired the great critic with more
even than his usual measure of sanity : and
perhaps the very best things in the Preface
and the notes are the frequent summonings
of ingenious sophistries to the bar of a merciless common sense. Let those who, with a
good living writer, fancy his criticism merely
a lifeless application of mechanical rules, read
again the famous passage in the preface where
he dismisses the claim of the unities of place
and time to be necessary to the proper illusion
of drama. Never did critic show himself freer
of the easy slavery to traditional rules which
afflicts or consoles sluggish minds. In Johnson's pages at any rate, there is " always an
appeal open," as he says, " from criticism to
nature." And, though all his prejudices,
except those of the Anti-Gallican, must have
carried him to the side of the unities, he goes
straight to the truth of experience, obtains
there a decisive answer, and records it in a few
pages of masterly reasoning. The first breath
of the facts, as known to every one who has
visited a theatre, is brought to demolish the
airy castles of pedantry : and it is shown that
unity is required not for the sake of deceiving

the spectators, which is impossible, but for the sake of bringing order into chaos, art into nature, and the immensity of life within limits that can be compassed by the powers of the human mind. The unity of action, which assists the mind, is therefore vital : the unities of time and place, which are apparently meant to deceive it, are empty impostures. For " the truth is that the spectators are always in their senses, and know, from the first act to the last, that the stage is only a stage and the players only players " : " the delight proceeds from our consciousness of fiction : if we thought murders and treasons real they would please no more."

But this is simply one specially famous passage in an essay which is full of matter from the first page to the last. It says little, of course, of the sublime poetry of Shakespeare, and it cannot anticipate that criticism of the imagination which Goethe and Coleridge have taught us to expect from every writer about Shakespeare. The day for that was not yet : and as Johnson, himself among the first to suggest the historical and comparative point of view in criticism, says in this very preface, " every man's performances, to be rightly estimated, must be compared with the state of the age in which he lived and with his own particular opportunities."

He had a different task, and he performed it so admirably that what he says can never be out of date. It had not then become superfluous to insist on the greatness of Shakespeare : if it has since become so no small share of that result may be ascribed to Johnson. We forget that, because, as he said of Dryden, it is the fate of a critic who convinces to be lost in the prevalence of his own discovery. Never certainly has the central praise of Shakespeare, as the master of truth and universality, been better set forth than by Johnson. Our ears are delighted, our powers of admiration quickened, our reasons convinced, as we read the succession of luminous and eloquent paragraphs in which he tries Shakespeare by the tests of time, of nature, of universality, and finds him supreme in all. Nor did Johnson ever write anything richer in characteristic and memorable sentences, fit to be quoted and thought over by themselves. " Nothing can please many and please long but just representations of general nature." " Shakespeare always makes nature predominant over accident. . . . His story requires Romans but he thinks only on men "; " there is a kind of intellectual remoteness necessary for the comprehension of any great work "; " nature (*i. e.* genius, what a man inherits at birth)

gives no man knowledge"; "upon the whole
all pleasure consists in variety"; "love has
no great influence upon the sum of life." It
is startling to find Johnson anticipating Mr.
Bernard Shaw, and more startling still to be
told in a study of the author of *Romeo and
Juliet* that love "has little operation in the
drama of a poet who caught his ideas from
the living world." But when we put ourselves in Johnson's position and compare
Shakespeare with the reigning dramatists of
France and England, we shall see that it is
in fact not the least striking thing about
Shakespeare that he has so many plays in
which the love interest scarcely appears.

The service Johnson rendered to the study
of Shakespeare is, however, by no means
confined to these general considerations. No
man did more, perhaps, to call criticism back
from paths that led to nowhere, or to suggest
directions in which discoveries might be made.
The most marked contrast between him and
earlier critics is his caution about altering the
received text. He first stemmed the tide of
rash emendation, and the ebb which began
with him has continued ever since. The case
for moderation in this respect has never been
better stated than in his words: "It has
been my settled principle that the reading of

the ancient books is probably true, and therefore is not to be disturbed for the sake of elegance, perspicuity or mere improvement of the sense. For though much credit is not due to the fidelity, nor any to the judgment of the first publishers, yet they who had the copy before their eyes were more likely to read it right than we who read it only by imagination." And in several other matters he in passing dropped a seed which has ripened in other minds to the great increase of our knowledge. " Shakespeare," he says, " has more allusions than other poets to the traditions and superstition of the vulgar, which must therefore be traced before he can be understood." Few critical seeds have had a larger growth than this : and the same may be said of the pregnant hint about the frequent necessity of looking for Shakespeare's meaning " among the sports of the field." He neither overestimated the importance nor underestimated the difficulties of the critic of Shakespeare. With his usual sense of the true scale of things he treats the quarrels of commentators with contempt : " it is not easy to discover from what cause the acrimony of a scholiast can naturally proceed. The subjects to be discussed by him are of very small importance : they involve neither property nor liberty "; and in another place

he characteristically bids his angry colleagues
to join with him in remembering amidst their
triumphs over the " nonsensical " opinions
of dead rivals that " we likewise are men :
that *debemur morti*, and, as Swift observed to
Burnet, we shall soon be among the dead ourselves." He knows too that " notes are
necessary evils " and advises the young reader
to begin by ignoring them and letting Shakespeare have his way alone. But at the same
time he puts aside with just indignation Pope's
supercilious talk about the " dull duty of an
editor " ; and after giving an admirable
summary of what that dull duty is, declares
that one part of it alone, the business of
conjectural criticism, "demands more than
humanity possesses." Yet it is that part of
his functions, the part which appeals most
to vanity, that he exercised with the most
sparing caution. He saw that it was not in
emendation but in interpretation that the
critic could now be most useful. For this
last task the sanity of his mind, though sometimes leaning too much to prose, gave him
peculiar qualifications. No one can have
used any of the Variorum Shakespeares without being struck again and again by the
masterly way in which Johnson penetrates
through the thicket of obscurities raised by
Shakespeare's involved language and his

critics' fanciful explanations, and brings back for us in plain words the undoubted meaning of many a difficult passage. He is a master of that rare art, the prose paraphrase of poetry. The perfect lucidity of his notes makes them always a pleasure to read : and writers of notes are not usually masters of language. Take such a note as that on the words of Laertes about Ophelia's madness—

> "Nature is fine in love : and, where 'tis fine,
> It sends some precious instance of itself
> After the thing it loves."

Johnson interprets : " love is the passion by which nature is most exalted and refined; and as substances, refined and subtilized, easily obey any impulse, or follow any attraction, some part of nature, so purified and refined, flies off after the attracting object, after the thing it loves ;—

> " As into air the purer spirits flow,
> And separate from their kindred dregs below,
> So flew her soul."

Nor can a mistake or two in details detract from the value of the splendid paraphrase of " To be or not to be," or the admirable note on the character of Polonius. Shakespeare has had subtler and more poetical critics than Johnson : but no one has equalled the insight, sobriety, lucidity and finality which Johnson shows in his own field.

The *Lives of the Poets* is Johnson's last, longest, and most popular work. More than any other of his works it was written to please himself : he did so much more than he was paid to do that he almost refuted his own doctrine that no man but a blockhead ever wrote except for money. Instead of being written, like most of his earlier books, in poverty, if not in obscurity, the *Lives* were written at his ease, with his pension in his pocket, with the booksellers at his feet, with the consciousness of an expectant and admiring public outside. The obstructions to his work were no longer those of poverty but of prosperity. He once had to write because if he did not he would starve : now he might sleep or talk all day with the certainty of sitting down to more meals than he wanted. In early life he had no temptation to quit his home, for he could not afford travel or amusement : now he could go to the Hebrides and talk of going further, without taking much thought of the expense. He once worked to make his name known : now his reputation was established and his name better known than he always found convenient. The result is that the *Lives* are easily written, full of anecdote and incident and manners, full of easily traceable allusions to himself and his own experiences, full of the magisterial decisions of a man whose judgments are no longer questioned, full, even more than usual, of frank confessions, open disregard of established opinion, the pleasant refusals of a wilful old man to reconsider his prejudices or take any more trouble about his work than he happens to choose. All this increases the readableness of the book. But it does not all increase its importance, and the fact is that not even the greatest of the *Lives* is as fine a piece of work as the Preface to the Shakespeare. Moreover, the work as a whole suffers from a disadvantage from which the Shakespeare is conspicuously exempt. It deals very largely with matters in which scarcely any one now takes any interest. In its three volumes Johnson gives us biographical and critical studies of fifty-two poets. Of these only six— Milton, Dryden, Pope, Thomson, Collins and Gray—would now be considered of first-rate poetic importance. Of the rest it is difficult to make certain of a dozen whose place in the second class would be unquestioned. The thirty or more that remain are mostly poets of whom the ordinary reader of to-day has never read, and if he is wise will never read, a single line. Great part of the book therefore is criticism not only upon the unimportant but upon what, so far as we are now concerned, may be called the non-existent. And even in Johnson's hands that cannot but mean barren writing and empty reading.

Yet the *Lives of the Poets* is not only the most popular book of its kind in the language : it is also a book of real and permanent value. No short Lives have ever equalled them. The most insignificant of the poets acquires a momentary interest as he passes through Johnson's hands. The art of biography is that of giving life to the dead : and that can only be done by the living. No one was ever more alive than Johnson. He says himself that he wrote his *Lives* unwillingly but with vigour and haste. The haste is apparent in a few places : the vigour everywhere. He had more pleasure in the biographical part of his work than in the critical, and consequently did it better. His strong love of life in all its manifestations prevented his ever treating an author merely as an author. He always goes straight to the man. And he knows that the individuality which makes the life of portraits is a matter of detail. Consequently he takes pains to record every detail that he can collect about his poets. The clothes of Milton, the chair Dryden occupied and its situation in summer and in winter, Pope's silver saucepan and potted lampreys, the reason why Addison sometimes absented himself from Button's, the remark which Swift made to Lord Orrery about a servant's faults in waiting at table and which Lord Orrery himself related to Johnson, these things and a hundred like them make Johnson's little biographies among the most vivid in the world. When once we have read them the poets they describe are for ever delivered from the remoteness of mere fame. Johnson has gone very close to them and he has taken us with him. And to have got close to men like Dryden, Pope, Swift and Addison is not among the smaller experiences of life. Two of them may indeed seem to us not to be poets at all, and the other two, possessing in such splendid abundance so many of a great poet's gifts, to have lacked the greatest and most essential of all : but great men the whole four undoubtedly were, among the greatest and most representative in the England of the century between the death of Milton and the birth of Wordsworth.

And Johnson belonged whole-heartedly to that century, lived in it, knew it more intimately perhaps than any man, believed in it and loved it without ever the shadow of a fear that there might be revolutionary surprises in store for the complacent self-assurance of its attitude towards literature, society and

life.   These were plainly unusual qualifications
for interpreting its great men to us.   And when
to these qualifications is added, as it was in
Johnson's case, a mind of great power, and
great pleasure in using its power, and a gift
of expression which has seldom been surpassed,
it is evident that a book like the *Lives* is certain
to be, what it is, one of the great monuments
and landmarks of our literature.   No literary
excursionist who has travelled to look at it
has ever regretted his journey.   For there is
in it the mind of a whole age : yet not fossilized
or mummified as in other hands it might so
easily have become by now, as the mind of
any age must soon become when it is left
entirely to itself.   Johnson did not leave it
entirely to itself.   It is true that in all matters
of political or literary controversy his mind was
narrowly imprisoned in the opinions of his own
or his father's age : and that is what makes
him such an admirable witness to them; but
here as elsewhere the life-giving quality in him
lies in his hold on the universal human things
which are affected by no controversies and
belong to all the ages.   None of his books
exhibit more of what he himself calls " the
two most engaging powers of an author."
In it " new things are made familiar and
familiar things are made new."   The famous
criticism of the " metaphysical poets " is so

written that a plain man feels at home in it : the thrice-told tale of the lives of Pope and Addison is so retold that every one thinks he reads it for the first time. The man who had in his earlier works sometimes seemed the most general and abstract even of eighteenth-century writers, becomes here, by force of his interest in the primary things of humanity, almost a pioneer of the new love of externalities, a relater of details, an anticipator of his own Boswell.

To the critical discussions he gave less space than to the lives, and no one will pretend to wish he had done the opposite. Allusion has already been made to his limitations as a critic of poetry. He was blind to the most poetic qualities of the greatest men : the purest poetry, the poetry that has refined away all but the absolutely indispensable minimum of prose alloy, often escaped him altogether, sometimes simply irritated his prejudices. *Omne ignotum pro injucundo.* He found people enthusiastic admirers of Milton's *Lycidas* or Gray's *Odes*, was angry at others enjoying what he found no pleasure in, and vented his temper on Gray and Milton. Though Collins was his friend he makes no mention of the *Ode to Evening*. In these cases and some others the critic is much less scrupulously fair than the biographer, to tell the truth, nearly

always is   There is perhaps a malicious touch
here and there in the lives of Milton, Swift and
Gray : but little as he liked any of them, how
fairly in each case the good points of the man
are brought out, and how they are left at
the end quite overbalancing the rest in our
memories !   But in the case of their works it
is different.   He has little to say about Gray's
Elegy, which he admired, and much about his
Odes, which he disliked.

Yet, in spite of some incapacity and some
unfairness, Johnson's criticism of poetry is
still a thing to be read with interest, profit
and admiration.   After all poetry is an art
as well as an inspiration : it may almost be
said to be a business as well as a pleasure.
There is still, when all has been said, that
indispensable alloy of prose in its composition
without which it crumbles into fragments, or
evaporates into mere mist.   The critical
questions which Horace and Boileau and
Pope discuss do not include the highest :
but they include much that no poet can put
aside as beneath him.   In this field Johnson
ranks among the masters of criticism.   His
mind did not travel outside its limits, but to
the work to be done within them it brought
knowledge, reflection, vigour and acuteness.
His reading had shown him how the writing
of verses, the construction of sentences, the

P

effective use of words, had advanced from the uncouthness and extravagance of the Elizabethans and Jacobeans to the amazing brevity, finish and dexterity of Pope. It is good for us to see it too with his eyes. We are apt to see only the beauty and truth that were lost in the process, and the mechanical clockwork that followed upon its completion. These he could not see : but we are in no danger of forgetting them, while we are in danger of forgetting that Pope's achievement gave us the most quotable verse that ever was written, and that his brilliancy and wit quickened the powers of expression of a whole nation. To understand this is well worth while : and Johnson helps us to understand it. Nor will the fact of his thinking that Pope improved upon Homer and that his translation is a model of melody, do us any harm : for we are not likely to follow him in either opinion.

As literary criticism the greatest of the *Lives* are those of Cowley, Dryden and Pope. But Johnson is not to be altogether despised even where he is plainly inadequate. Some of his strictures upon the poets whom he did not understand are sound enough in themselves : there is little to say against them except that they stand alone. The defect in his criticism of *Lycidas* is not that he attacks the mythological confusion of the poem—which is in fact

its weakness, not its strength ; but that he gives
no hint of sensibility to its haunting beauty of
phrase, of melody, of association, of passionate
feeling, not perhaps for its nominal subject,
but for the brief life of human friendship, for
the mingled tragedy of love and fame and
death. So again with Collins and Gray.
Johnson is perfectly right in saying that
Collins is too harsh and obscure, too apt to
lose his way " in quest of mistaken beauties " :
where he is wrong is in not saying that he
produced one of the most perfect Odes in our
own or any other language. And even in
Gray's case, where he is at his worst, there are
things which an intelligent lover of Gray is the
better for reading. There had been a good
deal of unintelligent and too promiscuous
admiration of Gray's *Odes* in Johnson's day :
and he performed a service, which is still a
service, by pointing out that there is in some
of their phrases a certain element of affectation
and artificiality. It is true, and still necessary
to be said, that Gray's " art and struggle are
too visible, and that there is in his *Odes* too
little appearance of ease and nature." The
object of criticism is the whole of truth : and
to see only the imaginative power, the metrical
learning and skill, the gift of language, the
gift of emotion, in Gray, is not to see the whole.
It is more important to see these things than

to see what Johnson saw : but in a complete criticism of Gray room must be found for an allusion to that element in him of which Johnson says, with some truth as well as malice : " he has a kind of strutting dignity and is tall by walking on tiptoe." In these matters we may listen with advantage to Johnson's instinct for reality; as we also may to his knowledge of the art of letters, when he points out quite truly that *Samson Agonistes* has no plot, and when he puts his finger at once on that central defect of *Paradise Lost* that " it comprises neither human actions nor human manners." That is too broadly stated no doubt : but it is true that the subject of poetry is the free play of human life, and that, from supernatural interference and from the peculiar position of Adam and Eve, there is far too little of this in *Paradise Lost*. Nor was it likely that a man of Johnson's learning and power of mind would confine himself in a book of this kind to the mere praise and blame of a succession of writers. That is his principal business : but of course he constantly overflows into general topics bearing upon literature or poetry as a whole. In these everybody who cares to think about the art of writing or analyse the pleasures of reading will find his account : they come in everywhere, of course. Now he makes some shrewd remarks,

not so much needed by the poets of his day
as by the novelists of our own, about the danger
of detailed enumeration by which description
so often loses all its power : for " of the greatest
things the parts are little." Now he is
incidentally laying down the true ideal of the
translator : to " exhibit his author's thoughts
in such a dress of diction as the author would
have given them, had his language been
English." Now he is discoursing at length
on what it was Wordworth's misfortune never
fully to understand, the immense power of
association upon words, so that the greatest
thoughts and noblest emotions fail of their
effect if expressed in words ordinarily connected
with trivial, vulgar, or ignoble actions, and
therefore necessarily arousing in the reader a
state of mind unfit for the reception of greatness. Or again he will speak of the value of
surprise in literature; " the pleasures of the
mind imply something sudden and unex-
pected." Or he will enlarge, as in the Life of
Addison, upon the definition of a simile, the
use of similes in poetry, and the distinction
between them and what he calls " exemplifi-
cations "; or, as in that of Pope, upon the
subject of representative metres and onoma-
topœic words. No one will pretend that all
he says in these general excursions is final :
but it is always the work of a man who had

read a great deal and had applied a very vigorous mind to what he had read. For all these reasons the *Lives of the Poets* will always be eagerly read by those who wish to understand a great man and a great period of English literature. But they will be read still more for their pleasantness, humanity and wisdom.

CHAPTER VI

THE FRIENDS OF JOHNSON

JOHNSON thought human life in general, and his own in particular, an unhappy business. Boswell once urged, in reply to his melancholy, that in fact life was lived upon the supposition of happiness : houses are built, gardens laid out, places of amusement erected and filled with company, and these things would not be done if people did not expect to enjoy themselves. As so often happens in these arguments Boswell appears to us to be substantially right. But the only reply he drew from Johnson was, " Alas, sir, these are all only struggles for happiness." And he went on to give a curious illustration of his rooted conviction that every man knew himself to be unhappy if he stopped to

think about it. "When I first entered
Ranelagh it gave an expansion and gay
sensation to my mind such as I never experienced anywhere else. But, as Xerxes wept
when he viewed his immense army and considered that not one of that great multitude
would be alive a hundred years afterwards,
so it went to my heart to consider that there
was not one in all that brilliant circle that
was not afraid to go home and think: but
that the thoughts of each individual there
would be distressing when alone." What he
thought was true of all men was certainly
true of himself. He hated and dreaded to
be alone. It was the pain of solitude quite
as much as the pleasure of society that drove
him abroad, and induced him to make a
business of keeping alive old friendships and
procuring new, till he had formed as large and
as interesting a circle of acquaintances as any
English man of letters has ever had.

That fact is an important element in his
fame. A great talker cannot exert his talent
in solitude; he cannot properly exert it except
in a society of intelligent men who can understand, appreciate, and in some degree contend
with him. Johnson would not have been the
wonderful talker he was if he had lived like
Richardson among gaping women and stupid

toadies. He did the very opposite. He lived among men several of whom possessed powers of mind quite as great as his own, however different, while their achievements seem to posterity decidedly greater than his. Our impression of his overwhelming distinction as a talker is not derived only from our own judgment as we read Boswell's record of it. It is derived almost as much from the fact that men so great as those he lived with acknowledged it with one accord. The primacy of Johnson was among them all an unquestioned article of faith. Hawkins, who knew him for so many years, says of him that " as Alexander and Cæsar were born for conquest, so was Johnson for the office of a symposiarch, to preside in all conversations "; and he adds, " I never yet saw the man who would venture to contest his right." But the greatest tribute came from the greatest of his friends. When Langdon, walking home one evening with Burke after both had dined in Johnson's company, regretted that Johnson had seized upon all the topics started by Burke, so that Burke himself had said little upon them, the reply of Burke is well known, " Oh, no; it is enough for me to have rung the bell to him." Such words from such a man are final and unanswerable. And they are confirmed by every other member of his inner circle, and indeed by almost every person who knew him and has left any opinion on the subject. Not the least significant tribute is that of those—including men no less great than Gibbon and Fox—who had not the courage to ring that dangerous bell which so often was brought down upon the head of the ringer. The " wonder and astonishment " he inspired were universal; and among those who really knew him they were commonly mingled with love. But whether there were love or not there was generally some degree of awe, even of actual fear, as apparently in the case of Gibbon. The unquestioned ascendency he possessed and exercised over men and women not accustomed to be over-awed is plainly written all over Boswell's story. The most celebrated of the scenes that prove or exhibit it is no doubt that of the signing of the " Round Robin " at Sir Joshua Reynolds's house in 1776, when a company which included, besides Reynolds himself, Burke, Gibbon, Sheridan, Colman, J. Warton, and Barnard, afterwards Bishop of Killaloe, were anxious to protest to Johnson against his proposed Latin Epitaph on Gold-smith; but not one dared to approach him about it or even to be the first to sign a letter to be sent to him. So a sailors' Round Robin, drawn up by Burke, was adopted, and all the signatures ran round it in equal daring. But the same thing appears perhaps even more curiously in a remark of Boswell's about a dinner at the house of Allan Ramsay. The company included Reynolds, Robertson the historian, Lord Binning and Boswell; and, Johnson being late in coming, they took to discussing him and his character. Soon, of course, he made his appearance; and then, says Boswell, "no sooner did he, of whom we had been thus talking so easily, arrive, than we were all as quiet as a school upon the entrance of the head-master." The best parallel perhaps to Johnson's position in his social world is that of the elder Pitt in Parliament. In each case the awe which was felt was much more than a mere vulgar fear of punishment; there was that in it, no doubt; but there was also a much rarer and finer thing; what we can only describe vaguely as a consciousness of the presence of greatness.

It is worth while to look a little more closely at the composition of this society in which Johnson reigned as unquestioned king. The most remarkable thing of all about it is that its inner and most intimate circle included four men of genius. Johnson had few or no closer friends than Reynolds, Burke, Goldsmith and Boswell. Of these the first two were acknowledged as the greatest

painter and the greatest orator then living
in England or perhaps in Europe; the third,
when he died, had some claim to be the truest
poet; and, what is more remarkable, the
lapse of over a hundred years has found little
or nothing to detract from the fame each
won from his contemporaries. Of Boswell
it is enough to repeat that, while he could not
compare with these men in life or action or
general powers of mind, and therefore enjoyed
no contemporary fame, he left a book behind
him at his death which every succeeding
generation has increasingly recognized as
possessing that uniqueness of achievement
which is another phrase for genius. Four
such men alone would make a society such
as few men have lived in. But Johnson's
society is as remarkable for the variety and
quantity, as for the quality, of its distinction.
No one can look through the invaluable index
of Dr. Birkbeck Hill's edition of Boswell
without being struck by this. If one were to
make a list of all the people whom Johnson
saw frequently or occasionally in the course
of his life it would include an astonishing
number of interesting names. Part of the
fascination of Boswell's book lies in that.
It is first and foremost the portrait of a man,
and everything is kept in subordination to
that. But it is also the picture of a whole

age and country. Sir Leslie Stephen remarked that nearly every distinguished man
of letters of that time came into contact with
Johnson. He mentions Hume and Gray as
the only exceptions. There may be others,
as for instance Sterne, to be added. But it
remains true that Johnson was in exceptionally close personal touch with the whole
literary world of his day. And Boswell has
known how to make use of all that to give
interest and variety to his book. Nor was
Johnson ever, as we have seen, a mere narrow
man of letters. He had a universal curiosity
about life and men. He could talk to every
one, and every one found his talk interesting.
Consequently Boswell's record of his acquaintance is by no means a mere series of literary
portraits. The society is of all the sorts of
men and women that intelligent men can
care to meet, the talk on almost all the
subjects which such people can care to
discuss.

Let us glance at some of the names that
would find places in that list. We may begin
with the statesmen. There is first of all
Shelburne, who was Prime Minister the year
before Johnson died; the most mysterious
figure in the politics of that day, George III's
Jesuit of Berkeley Square, the " Malagrida "
of the pamphleteers, to whom Goldsmith

made his well-known unfortunate remark, "I never could conceive the reason why they call you Malagrida, for Malagrida was a very good sort of man." But for all this sinister reputation he was certainly an able and interesting man. He was a great patron of the arts, a princely collector of manuscripts, and an unusually enlightened student of politics if not a great statesman. How intimately Johnson knew him is, like almost everything about Shelburne, uncertain; but it is known that they used to meet in London and that Johnson once at least was Shelburne's guest at Bowood. A greater man who was never Prime Minister was a much more intimate friend. Fox talked little before Johnson; and the two men were as different in many ways as men could be. Of the two it was certainly not the professed man of letters who was the greater lover of literature. But Fox was a member of "The Club," and an intimate friend of Burke and Reynolds, and in these ways he and Johnson often met. In spite of all differences each made a great impression on the other. Fox indignantly defended Johnson's pension in the House of Commons so early as 1774, and the last book read to him, except the Church Service, was Johnson's *Lives of the Poets*. Johnson was like the rest of the world dazzled by the daring

parliamentary genius of Fox, and said that
he had "divided the kingdom with Cæsar
so that there was a doubt whether the nation
should be ruled by the sceptre of George III
or the tongue of Fox." He was for the King
against Fox, because the King was his
"master," but for Fox against Pitt because
"Fox is my friend."

Another contemporary statesman who was
intimate with Johnson was the cultivated
and high-minded William Windham. No
one had a greater reverence for Johnson.
The most scrupulous of men, he was probably
attracted to Johnson most of all by his
character, and sought in him a kind of director
for his conscience. Johnson, however, disapproved of scruples, and when Windham
expressed, as Boswell says, "some modest
and virtuous doubts" whether he ought to
accept the post of Secretary to the Lord
Lieutenant of Ireland because of the dubious
practices supposed to be necessary to the
holding of that office, all the answer he got
was "a pleasant smile" and "Don't be
afraid, sir, you will soon make a very pretty
rascal." But Windham took no discourage-
ments and was to the end one of Johnson's
most devoted disciples. He put such a
value on Johnson's society that he once rode
forty miles out of his way on a journey in

order to get a day and a half with him at Ashbourne : and he was one of the little band of friends who constantly visited the dying man in the last days of his life. One day when he had placed a pillow to support the old man's head, Johnson thanked him and said, "That will do—all that a pillow can do." He was one of the pall-bearers at the funeral.

A less famous political friend was William Gerard Hamilton, with whom he at one time engaged in political work of some sort serious enough to induce him to write a special prayer about it. "Single speech Hamilton," as he was called, behaved badly to Burke and was, it seems, widely distrusted; but Johnson maintained a life-long friendship with him, and had a high opinion of his conversational powers. Hamilton in return thought that he found in Johnson, when not talking for victory, a "wisdom not only convincing but overpowering"; and showed his gratitude by placing his purse at Johnson's disposal when he supposed him to be in want of money. It was he—a man of public business and affairs all his life—who said of Johnson's death that it had "made a chasm which not only nothing can fill up, but which nothing has a tendency to fill up. Johnson is dead. Let us go to the next best : there is nobody; no man can be said to put you in mind of Johnson." So also thought another member of Parliament, George Dempster, whom Burns honoured with his praise. He once told Boswell not to think of his health, but to sit up all night listening to Johnson; for "one had better be palsied at eighteen than not keep company with such a man." Another politician in his circle was Fitz-Herbert, a man of whom Burke had the highest opinion, and of whom Johnson made the curious remark that he was the most "acceptable of men because his good qualities were negative and he offended no one." Fitz-Herbert spoke of Johnson in the House of Commons as his friend and called him "a pattern of morality."

Two other well-known political figures may be mentioned as acquaintances of Johnson; both men of more ability than character. Lord Chancellor Thurlow was a type of the lawyer who fights his way to success and cares for little else. But he was a true and generous friend to Johnson, for whose proposed journey to Italy he offered to provide the means. And if his career allowed any one to think meanly of his abilities, Johnson's opinion of them would be a sufficient answer. He always maintained that "to make a speech in a public assembly is a knack"; it was the question and answer of conversation, he thought, that showed what a man's real abilities were. And out of that test Thurlow came so triumphantly that Johnson said of him, " I would prepare myself for no man in England but Lord Thurlow. When I am to meet with him I should wish to know a day before." He paid him the same compliment more than once; and the man to whom he paid it cannot have been the least interesting element in that interesting circle. A very different figure was the infidel and demagogue Wilkes, of whom Johnson had used the most violent language in public and private, but with whom, under the dexterous management of Boswell, he came to be on terms of friendly acquaintance. The story of how Boswell brought them together, of which Burke said that there was " nothing to equal it in the whole history of the *Corps Diplomatique*," is one of the very best things in the *Life*. Of course they never became friendly, but they met occasionally and Johnson sent Wilkes a presentation copy of his *Lives*. The acquaintance is one of the most striking instances of the real tolerance which lay behind Johnson's outbursts of prejudice. He and Wilkes had nothing in common but quick brains, witty tongues, social gifts and dislike of the Scotch; but that was enough.

Q

Johnson would have sympathized with the respectable freeholder of Middlesex who, when canvassed for his vote by Wilkes replied, " Vote for you, sir ! I would rather vote for the devil ! " But he would have sympathized even more with the candidate's reply : " But —in case your friend does not stand ? "

No one will say that a set of acquaintances which stretched from Burke at one end to Wilkes at the other did not provide strong and varied political meat for the society to which they belonged. It is just the same when we look beyond politics. If all Johnson's acquaintances could have been gathered into one room, the unlikeliest people would have found themselves together. The saintly John Wesley, for instance, and the very far from saintly Topham Beauclerk, make a curious pair. Yet both of them loved and honoured Johnson all their lives and both were always loved, at any rate, by him; and the one who got the less honour got the more love. No one could take such liberties with Johnson as this man who had been through the Divorce Court and was behaving badly to the wife whom he had stolen. Johnson did not spare Beauclerk the rebukes he deserved : but he could not resist the intellectual gifts and social charm of that true descendant of Charles II. When Beauclerk

lay dying Johnson said, " I would walk to
the extent of the diameter of the earth to
save Beauclerk "; and when he was dead,
Johnson wrote to Boswell, " Poor dear Beauclerk—*nec, ut soles, dabis joca.*" That he
could win the warm affection of such a man
as Beauclerk is one more proof of the breadth
of his sympathies. The most surprising people
felt his fascination. Wraxall says that he
had seen the beautiful Duchess of Devonshire, " then in the first bloom of youth,
hanging on the sentences that fell from Johnson's lips, and contending for the nearest
place to his chair "; and it is recorded of
Kitty Clive the actress, whom he used to go
and see in the green-room, that she said of
him, " I love to sit by Dr. Johnson : he
always entertains me."

But of course neither Duchesses, nor
actresses, nor even gay young men of fashion
fresh from the Divorce Court, were more
than occasional or single splendours in the
Johnsonian heaven : its fixed stars of ordinary
nights were less dazzling persons. Many were
scholars, of course, as befitted a man of books.
The greatest, but one of the least frequent or
intimate, was Gibbon. He was a member of
"The Club" and a friend of Reynolds and
Fox : but his feeling for Johnson was apparently one of fear unmingled with love. Though

he met them both fairly often, he never mentions Boswell, and Johnson only once or twice. The historian who could not talk was not likely to appreciate the great talker who cared nothing for history: so one is not surprised to find Johnson dismissed in the famous *Memoirs* as merely the "oracle" of Reynolds. A much greater friend was another member of "The Club," Percy, of the *Reliques of Poetry*, afterwards a Bishop, with whom he often quarrelled but was always reconciled. Boswell managed the most important of their reconciliations by obtaining a letter from Johnson testifying to Percy's merit which so pleased Percy that he said, "I would rather have this than degrees from all the Universities in Europe." The whole story is a curious proof of the respect in which Johnson was held: for Percy's grievance was that Johnson had snubbed him in the presence of a distinguished member of his own family, "to whom he hoped to have appeared more respectable by showing how intimate he was with Dr. Johnson." Johnson laughed at Percy's ballads and would have been the last person to guess the immense influence the publication of the *Reliques* was to have on the development of English literature in the next century: but he knew his value, and said he never met him without learning something from him.

Among other men of interest with whom he may be said to have been intimate at one time or another in his life may be mentioned his old pupil David Garrick, the most famous and perhaps the greatest of English actors, whom he loved and abused and would allow no one else to abuse: Richardson, the author of *Clarissa*, who once came to his rescue when he was arrested for debt, and of whose powers he had such a high opinion that he declared that there was " more knowledge of the heart in one letter of Richardson's than in all *Tom Jones* "; the two Wartons, Joseph, the Headmaster of Winchester and editor of Pope, and Thomas the author of the history of English Poetry and himself Poet Laureate; both good scholars and critics who partly anticipated the poetic tastes of the nineteenth century: Paoli, the hero of Boswell and the Corsicans, with whom Johnson loved to dine: Douglas, Bishop of Salisbury, who wrote against Hume and edited Clarendon; Savage, the poet of mysterious birth whose homeless life he sometimes shared and finally recorded: George Psalmanazar, the converted impostor, an even more mysterious person, whom Johnson reverenced and said he " sought after " more than any man: booksellers like Cave and Davies and the brothers Dilly: scholarly lawyers like Sir William Scott, afterwards

Lord Stowell, whom he made executor to his will, and Sir Robert Chambers whom he reproved for tossing snails over a wall into his neighbour's garden till he heard the neighbour was a Dissenter, on which he said, "Oh, if so, toss away, Chambers, toss away"; and physicians like Heberden, beloved of Cowper, whom Johnson called *ultimus Romanorum*, and Laurence, President of the College of Physicians, to whom he addressed a Latin Ode. All these were men of interest either in themselves or in their experience of life; all brought something worth having to the society in which they lived; and with all of them Johnson may be said to have been on intimate terms. Nor did he confine his friendship to men. He had a higher opinion of the intellectual capacities of women than most men of his time, and many of the most remarkable women of the time enjoyed his intimacy. Among them may be mentioned Elizabeth Carter, the translator of Epictetus, whom he thought the best Greek scholar he had known, and praised for being also a good maker of puddings; Fanny Burney, of whose novels he was an enthusiastic admirer; Mrs. Montagu, Mrs. Macaulay, and Hannah More, the chief learned ladies of the day, all three women of real ability; and his own brilliant and witty Mrs. Thrale, who without being a professed "blue stocking" has for Johnson's sake and her own quite eclipsed the "blue stockings" in the interest of posterity. Altogether it is an astonishing list. Johnson never thought of himself as a man to be envied; but if man is a social being, and no man was so more than Johnson, there can be few things more enviable, in possession or in retrospect, than the society, the friendship, or, as it often was, the love, of such men and women as these.

If we go further and extend the inquiry to those who can scarcely be called intimate friends, but with whom he was brought into more or less frequent social contact, the list becomes, of course, too long to give. But it may be worth while to mention that it would again include a very large number of men who had something in them above the ordinary. For instance, so great a name as that of Hogarth would be found in it, making with Allan Ramsay whom he also knew well and Reynolds who was perhaps the most intimate of all his friends, a remarkable trio to gather round a man who cared nothing for painting. He managed without that to impress them so much that Reynolds gave the credit of whatever was best in his *Discourses* to the "education" he had had under Johnson: and Hogarth declared that his conversation was to the talk

of other men " like Titian's painting compared
to Hudson's." This outer circle includes also
distinguished architects like Sir William
Chambers who built Somerset House, and
Gwynn who built Magdalen Bridge at Oxford
and the English bridge at Shrewsbury: bishops
like Barnard of Killaloe, and Shipley the liberal
and reforming bishop of St. Asaph : poets like
Collins and Young: historians and divines
like Robertson and Hugh Blair : philosophers
and men of science like Adam Smith and Sir
Joseph Banks : with a certain number of
intelligent peers like Lord Orrery the friend
of Swift, Lord Marchmont the friend of Pope,
and Lord Elibank whom Smollett praised for
his " universal intelligence " and who said,
when he was already seventy, that he would
go five hundred miles to enjoy a day in Johnson's company; besides public men like Lord
Charlemont the Irish statesman and traveller
who once went to visit Montesquieu, and Lord
Macartney who had gone as ambassador to
Russia and was soon to go in the same position
to Pekin.

It is unnecessary to extend the list. All
these men knew Johnson to a greater or less
extent, and added to the interest of his life,
as they add to the interest of Boswell's record
of it. Many or most of them are known to
have recognized the greatness of Johnson.

The words of some have been quoted and others might easily be added. Johnson often appears great in the books he wrote, and often too in the books which others have written about him : but it seems certain that unlike most authors he was far greater in bodily presence than he can be in his own or any one else's books. Even Boswell's magic pen cannot quite equal the living voice. To the overpowering impression made by that voice upon those who heard it, sometimes of almost bodily fear, oftener of a delight that could not have enough, always of amazed astonishment, the testimonies are not only innumerable, but so strongly worded and so evidently sincere as to suggest the conclusion that the fortunate listeners are attempting to relate an experience unique in the world's history. Even those who had suffered from his rudeness like Wraxall, the author of the well-known *Memoirs*, give the impression of being unable to find words strong enough to describe the power of his presence, so that they use expressions like the " compass of his gigantic faculties " and " the sublime attainments of his mind " in speaking of the gap felt by the company when he left a room. The latter expression at any rate hardly seems to us exactly to fit Johnson ; but no doubt Wraxall uses the word " sublime " because he wants to imply that there was something in Johnson's talk utterly out of the reach of ordinary men of ability. In fact it does seem probable that no recorded man has ever talked with Johnson's amazing freedom and power. Such an assertion cannot be proved, of course; but it would be difficult to exaggerate the weight of the evidence pointing in that direction. We have seen the kind of society in which he lived. In that society, rich in so many kinds of distinction, he was always accorded, as his right, a kind of informal but quite undisputed precedence. And it seems to have been the same among strangers as soon as he had opened his mouth. Whenever and whereever tongues were moving his primacy was immediate and unquestioned. The actual ears that could hear him were necessarily few; no man's acquaintances can be more than an insignificant fraction of the public. But in his case they were sufficiently numerous, distinguished and enthusiastic to send the fame of his talk all over the country. Is he the only man whose "Bon Mots," as they were called, have been published in his lifetime? "A mighty impudent thing," as he said of it, but also an irrefragable proof of his celebrity. And on the whole his popularity, then and since, has equalled his fame   Much is said of his rudeness and violence, but the fact remains that in all his life it does not appear to have cost him a single friend except the elder Sheridan. Those who knew him best bear the strongest testimony to the fundamental goodness of his heart. Reynolds said that he was always the first to seek a reconciliation, Goldsmith declared that he had nothing of the bear but his skin, and Boswell records many instances of his placability after a quarrel. The love his friends felt for him is written large all over Boswell's pages. And of that feeling the public outside came more and more to share as much as strangers could. Even in his lifetime he began to receive that popular canonization which has been developing ever since. Perhaps the most curious of all the proofs of this is the fact mentioned by Boswell in a note, "that there were copper pieces struck at Birmingham with his head impressed on them, which pass current as halfpence there, and in the neighbouring parts of the country." Has that ever happened to any other English writer ? Well may Boswell cite it in evidence of Johnson's extraordinary popularity. It is that and it is more. There is in it not merely a tribute of affection to the living and speaking man, there is also an anticipation of the most remarkable thing about his subsequent fame. That has had all along, as we saw at first, a popular element in it. It has never been, like that of most scholars and critics, an exclusively literary thing, confined solely to people of literary instincts. Rather it has been, more and more, what the newspapers and the *Johnsoniana* and these coins or medals already suggested, something altogether wider. Samuel Johnson was in his lifetime a well-known figure in the streets, a popular name in the press. He is now a national institution, with the merits, the defects, and the popularity which belong to national institutions. His popularity is certainly not diminished by the fact that he was the complacent victim of many of our insular prejudices and exhibited a good deal of the national tendency to a crude and self-confident Philistinism. These things come so humanly from him that his wisest admirers have scarcely the heart to complain or disapprove. They laugh at him, and with him, and love him still. But they could not love him as they do if he embodied only the weaknesses of his race. The position he holds in their affection, and the affection of the whole nation, is due to other and greater qualities. It is these that have given him his rare and indeed unique distinction as the accepted and traditional spokesman of the integrity, the humour, and the obstinate common sense, of the English people.

BIBLIOGRAPHY

The finest Library Edition of the complete works of Johnson is that published at Oxford in nine volumes in 1825. Another good one, the volumes of which are less heavy, is that of 1823 in twelve volumes, edited by Alexander Chalmers.

Among the very numerous editions of particular works the following may be mentioned—

The Six Chief Lives from Johnson's "Lives of the Poets"; with Macaulay's "Life of Johnson." Edited, with a Preface by MATTHEW ARNOLD. 1878.

History of Rasselas, Prince of Abyssinia. Edited, with Introduction and Notes by GEORGE BIRKBECK HILL. 1887.

Lives of the English Poets. By SAMUEL JOHNSON, LL.D. Edited by GEORGE BIRKBECK HILL, D.C.L. In three volumes. 1905.

Johnson on Shakespeare. Essays and Notes selected and set forth with an Introduction. By WALTER RALEIGH. 1908.

The Letters of Samuel Johnson, LL.D. Collected and edited by GEORGE BIRKBECK HILL. In two volumes. 1892.

Only a few of the letters are given in the editions of the complete works. In this edition the letters already given by Boswell in his *Life* are not reprinted.

Select Essays of Dr. Johnson. Edited by GEORGE BIRKBECK HILL. In two volumes. 1889. (Temple Library.)

These Essays are chiefly from *The Rambler* and *The Idler.*

Wit and Wisdom of Samuel Johnson. Selected and arranged by GEORGE BIRKBECK HILL. 1888.

This consists of sayings on various subjects arranged alphabetically, with an interesting introduction.

The main authority for the life of Johnson is, of course, Boswell. His account is given in two books, the *Journal of a Tour to the Hebrides with Samuel Johnson, LL.D.*, published in 1785, and the *Life* which followed in two volumes in 1791.

The best edition of the *Life* is that edited by Dr. Birkbeck Hill in six volumes, one of which is given to the *Tour to the Hebrides*, published in 1887. No one who has worked on Johnson since that year can overstate his debt to this book or his gratitude to its author. The prettiest and pleasantest of all editions of Boswell is that known as Wright's Croker. It is a revision by J. Wright of the edition by J. W. Croker, and includes a collection of Johnsoniana. It consists of ten handy volumes, illustrated by many steel engravings, and first appeared in 1831.

The most important of the many accounts of Johnson left by other contemporaries are those given by Mrs. Thrale, Fanny Burney and his executor, Sir John Hawkins. Mrs. Thrale's is contained in a volume entitled *Anecdotes of the late Samuel Johnson, LL.D., during the last Twenty Years of his Life. By Hester Lynch Piozzi.* It was first published in 1786. Fanny Burney's picture of him is to be found in her *Diary and Letters*, of which the best edition is that by Austin Dobson, 1904. Sir John Hawkins prefixed a Life of Johnson to the edition of his works which he brought out in 1787. Dr. Birkbeck Hill has reprinted a large collection of biographical matter drawn from a variety of sources in his two volumes of *Johnsonian Miscellanies*, 1897.

The critical studies of Johnson are of course innumerable. Among the best are Carlyle's, printed in his *Works* among the *Miscellaneous Essays*, Sir Leslie Stephen's volume in the "English Men of Letters" series, and Sir Walter Raleigh's *Six Essays on Johnson*. The *Life* written by Macaulay for the *Encyclopædia Britannica* and reprinted by Matthew Arnold in his edition of the *Six Chief Lives* must not be confused with the essay reprinted in the collected Essays.

Dr. Birkbeck Hill published in 1879 an edition of Boswell's correspondence with the Hon. A. Erskine, and of his *Journal of a Tour to Corsica*, reprinted from the original editions. Boswell's Letters to his and Gray's friend, the Rev. J. W. Temple, were first published in 1857.

INDEX

(Principally of Persons known to Dr. Johnson, or mentioned in his Writings or Conversation)

THE HOME UNIVERSITY
LIBRARY *of Modern Knowledge*

Edited by Professors J. Arthur Thomson, Gilbert Murray, H. A. L. Fisher and W. T. Brewster.

Comprehensive and authoritative volumes on every prominent educational and cultural subject. The books are cloth bound, printed on high grade paper, with bibliographies, indices, and illustrations, charts and maps where needed. Jackets in two colors. Each volume complete and sold separately. *Per volume,* **One Dollar.**

(*ORDER BY NUMBER*)

AMERICAN HISTORY

[*Order Number*]

25. **THE CIVIL WAR (1854-1865). By Frederick L. Paxson,** Professor of American History, University of Wisconsin.

39. **RECONSTRUCTION AND UNION (1865-1912). By Paul Leland Haworth.** A History of the United States in our own times.

47. **THE COLONIAL PERIOD (1607-1766). By Charles McLean Andrews,** Professor of American History, Yale.

67. **FROM JEFFERSON TO LINCOLN (1815-1860). By William MacDonald,** Professor of History, Brown University. The author makes the history of this period circulate about constitutional ideas and slavery sentiment.

82. **THE WARS BETWEEN ENGLAND AND AMERICA (1763-1815). By Theodore C. Smith,** Professor of American History, Williams College. A history of the period, with especial emphasis on The Revolution and The War of 1812.

GENERAL HISTORY AND GEOGRAPHY

3. **THE FRENCH REVOLUTION. By Hilaire Belloc.**

4. **A SHORT HISTORY OF WAR AND PEACE. By G. H. Perris**, author of "Russia in Revolution," etc.

7. **MODERN GEOGRAPHY. By Dr. Marion Newbigin.** Shows the relation of physical features to living things and to some of the chief institutions of civilization.

8. **POLAR EXPLORATION. By Dr. W. S. Bruce,** leader of the "Scotia" expedition. Emphasizes the results of the expedition.

13. **MEDIEVAL EUROPE. By H. W. C. Davis,** Fellow at Balliol College, Oxford, author of "Charlemagne," etc.

18. **THE OPENING UP OF AFRICA. By Sir H. H. Johnston.**

19. **THE CIVILIZATION OF CHINA. By H. A. Giles,** Professor of Chinese, Cambridge.

20. **HISTORY OF OUR TIME (1885-1911). By C. P. Gooch.**

22. **THE PAPACY AND MODERN TIMES. By Rev. William Barry, D.D.,** author of "The Papal Monarchy," etc. The story of the rise and fall of the Temporal Power.

26. **THE DAWN OF HISTORY. By J. L. Myers,** Professor of Ancient History, Oxford.

30. **ROME. By W. Warde Fowler,** author of "Social Life at Rome," etc.

33. **THE HISTORY OF ENGLAND. By A. F. Pollard,** Professor of English History, University of London.

34. **CANADA. By A. G. Bradley.**

36. **PEOPLES AND PROBLEMS OF INDIA. By Sir T. W. Holderness.** "The best small treatise dealing with the range of subjects fairly indicated by the title."—*The Dial.*

51. **MASTER MARINERS. By John R. Spears,** author of "The History of Our Navy," etc. A history of sea craft adventure from the earliest times.

LITERATURE AND ART

NATURAL SCIENCE

9. **THE EVOLUTION OF PLANTS. By Dr. D. H. Scott,** President of the Linnean Society of London. The story of the development of flowering plants, from the earliest zoological times, unlocked from technical language.

12. **THE ANIMAL WORLD. By Prof. F. W. Gamble.**

14. **EVOLUTION. By Prof. J. Arthur Thomson and Prof. Patrick Geddes.** Explains to the layman what the title means to the scientific world.

15. **INTRODUCTION TO MATHEMATICS. By A. N. Whitehead,** author of "Universal Algebra."

17. **CRIME AND INSANITY. By Dr. C. Mercier,** author of "Crime and Criminals," etc.

21. **AN INTRODUCTION TO SCIENCE. By Prof. J. Arthur Thomson,** Science Editor of the Home University Library. For those unacquainted with the scientific volumes in the series this should prove an excellent introduction.

23. **ASTRONOMY. By A. R. Hinks,** Chief Assistant at the Cambridge Observatory. "Decidedly original in substance, and the most readable and informative little book on modern astronomy we have seen for a long time."— *Nature.*

24. **PSYCHICAL RESEARCH. By Prof. W. F. Barrett,** formerly President of the Society for Psychical Research.

37. **ANTHROPOLOGY. By R. R. Marett,** Reader in Social Anthropology, Oxford. Seeks to plot out and sum up the general series of changes, bodily and mental, undergone by man in the course of history. "Excellent. So enthusiastic, so clear and witty, and so well adapted to the general reader."—*American Library Association Booklist.*

41. **PSYCHOLOGY, THE STUDY OF BEHAVIOUR. By William McDougall,** of Oxford. A well-digested summary of the essentials of the science put in excellent literary form by a leading authority.

42. **THE PRINCIPLES OF PHYSIOLOGY. By Prof. J. G. McKendrick.** A compact statement by the Emeritus Professor at Glasgow, for uninstructed readers.

116. **EUGENICS. By A. M. Carr-Saunders.** Biological problems, together with the facts and theories of heredity.

119. **GAS AND GASES. By R. M. Caven, D.Sc., F.I.C.,** Royal Technical College, Glasgow. The chemical and physical nature of gases, both in their scientific and historical aspects.

122. **BIRDS, AN INTRODUCTION TO ORNITHOL-OGY. By A. L. Thompson, O.B.E., D.Sc.** A general account of the characteristics, mainly of habit and behavior of birds.

124. **SUNSHINE AND HEALTH. By Ronald Campbell Macfie, M.B.C.M., LL.D.** Light and its relation to man treated scientifically.

126. **TREES. By MacGregor Skene, D.Sc., F.L.S.** Senior Lecturer on Botany, Bristol University. A concise study of the classification, history, structure, architecture, growth, enemies, care and protection of trees. Forestry and economics are also discussed.

PHILOSOPHY AND RELIGION

35. **THE PROBLEMS OF PHILOSOPHY. By Bertrand Russell,** Lecturer and Late Fellow Trinity College, Cambridge.

44. **BUDDHISM. By Mrs. Rhys Davids,** Lecturer on Indian Philosophy, Manchester.

46. **ENGLISH SECTS: A HISTORY OF NONCON-FORMITY. By W. B. Selbie,** Principal of Manchester College, Oxford.

50. **THE MAKING OF THE NEW TESTAMENT. By B. W. Bacon,** Professor of New Testament Criticism, Yale. An authoritative summary of the results of modern critical research with regard to the origins of the New Testament.

52. **ETHICS. By G. E. Moore,** Lecturer in Moral Science, Cambridge. Discusses what is right and what is wrong, and the whys and wherefores.

55. **MISSIONS: THEIR RISE AND DEVELOPMENT. By Mrs. Mandell Creighton,** author of "History of England." The author seeks to prove that missions have done more to civilize the world than any other human agency.

60. **COMPARATIVE RELIGION. By Prof. J. Estlin Carpenter.** "One of the few authorities on this subject compares all the religions to see what they have to offer on the great themes of religion."—*Christian Work and Evangelist.*

65. **THE LITERATURE OF THE OLD TESTAMENT. By George F. Moore,** Professor of the History of Religion, Harvard University. "A popular work of the highest order. Will be profitable to anybody who cares enough about Bible study to read a serious book on the subject."—*American Journal of Theology.*

69. **A HISTORY OF FREEDOM OF THOUGHT. By John B. Bury, M.A., LL.D.,** Regius Professor of Modern History in Cambridge University. Summarizes the history of the long struggle between authority and reason and of the emergence of the principle that coercion of opinion is a mistake.

88. **RELIGIOUS DEVELOPMENT BETWEEN OLD AND NEW TESTAMENTS. By R. H. Charles,** Canon of Westminster. Shows how religious and ethical thought between 180 B. C. and 100 A. D. grew naturally into that of the New Testament.

96. **A HISTORY OF PHILOSOPHY. By Clement C. J. Webb,** *Oxford.*

SOCIAL SCIENCE

1. **PARLIAMENT. ITS HISTORY, CONSTITUTION, AND PRACTICE. By Sir Courtenay P. Ilbert**, Clerk of the House of Commons.

5. **THE STOCK EXCHANGE. By F. W. Hirst**, Editor of the London *Economist*. Reveals to the nonfinancial mind the facts about investment, speculation, and the other terms which the title suggests.

6. **IRISH NATIONALITY. By Mrs. J. R. Green.** A brilliant account of the genius and mission of the Irish people. "An entrancing work, and I would advise everyone with a drop of Irish blood in his veins or a vein of Irish sympathy in his heart to read it."—*New York Times Review.*

10. **THE SOCIALIST MOVEMENT. By J. Ramsay Macdonald**, Chairman of the British Labor Party.

11. **THE SCIENCE OF WEALTH. By J. A. Hobson**, author of "Problems of Poverty." A study of the structure and working of the modern business world.

16. **LIBERALISM. By Prof. L. T. Hobhouse**, author of "Democracy and Reaction." A masterly philosophical and historical review of the subject.

28. **THE EVOLUTION OF INDUSTRY. By D. H. MacGregor**, Professor of Political Economy, University of Leeds. An outline of the recent changes that have given us the present conditions of the working classes and the principles involved.

29. **ELEMENTS OF ENGLISH LAW. By W. M. Geldart**, Vinerian Professor of English Law, Oxford. A simple statement of the basic principles of the English legal system on which that of the United States is based.

32. **THE SCHOOL: AN INTRODUCTION TO THE STUDY OF EDUCATION. By J. J. Findlay**, Professor of Education, Manchester. Presents the history, the psychological basis, and the theory of the school with a rare power of summary and suggestion.

49. **ELEMENTS OF POLITICAL ECONOMY. By S. J. Chapman**, Professor of Political Economy and Dean of Faculty of Commerce and Administration, University of Manchester.

Published by

HENRY HOLT AND COMPANY

One Park Avenue   New York